MACHO
NACHOS

MACHO

50 TOPPINGS, SALSAS, AND SPREADS FOR IRRESISTIBLE SNACKS AND LIGHT MEALS

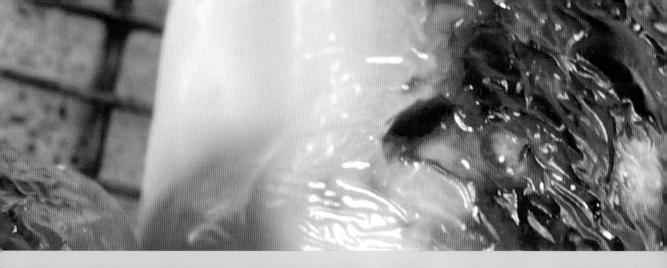

NACHOS

CLARKSON POTTER/PUBLISHERS · NEW YORK

KATE HEYHOE

PHOTOGRAPHS BY THOMAS WAY AND KATE HEYHOE

TO JOHN "HANK" DOONAN

Remember Beto, La Cumbia, and starry longneck nights at Liberty Lunch? Good nachos and great times. I'm so glad we shared them together. Keep on truckin', big brother.

ACKNOWLEDGMENTS

Food—writing about it, making it, and eating it—should be a joy. Thanks to all who've given me the chance to have more fun with this book than a day at a dude ranch: Chris Pavone, my editor; Lisa Ekus, my agent; and all the brilliant folks at Clarkson Potter who infused my little manuscript with mucho machismo (especially Jan Derevjanik). Most of all, thanks to my partner in everything, Thomas Way, for his patience, genius, and exceedingly good taste.

Text copyright © 2003 by Kate Heyhoe
Photographs copyright © 2003 by Thomas Way and Kate Heyhoe

Published by Clarkson Potter/Publishers, New York, New York. Member of the Crown Publishing Group, a division of Random House, Inc.
www.randomhouse.com

CLARKSON N. POTTER is a trademark and POTTER and colophon are registered trademarks of Random House, Inc.

Printed in Singapore

Design by Jan Derevjanik

Library of Congress Cataloging-in-Publication Data
Heyhoe, Kate.
     Macho nachos : 50 toppings, salsas, and spreads for irresistible snacks and light meals / Kate Heyhoe ; photographs by Thomas Way and Kate Heyhoe.
     1. Nachos. I. Title.
     TX740.H49   2003
     641.8'12—dc21   2003004336

ISBN 1-4000-5042-1

10 9 8 7 6 5 4 3 2 1

First Edition

CONTENTS

INTRODUCTION:
THE EVOLUTION OF A REVOLUTION

Don't confuse nachos with the gooey, gloppy orange stuff served in ballparks and cheap restaurants. Real nachos are macho: They're topped with fresh, natural ingredients, tangy cheeses, heady spices, and hearty beans, meats, or seafood. Real men may eat quiche, but real people—from truck drivers to movie stars— eat real nachos.

The original melted cheese–and–jalapeño nacho originated in Piedras Negras, along the Rio Grande border, during World War II. The concoction, named after its inventor Ignacio "Nacho" Anaya, quickly jumped the border, blazing through Texas and across the rest of the nation like wildfire. Oil billionaires, Texas governors, and U.S. presidents have all feasted on this authentic Tex-Mex snack, and to this day it never goes out of style. I've slurped up bean 'n' cheese nachos in dark Mexican bars, but I've also been served crab and spinach nachos on silver platters by white-gloved butlers at the mansions of our nation's richest oilmen. Nachos cut across class, sex, and income. They're simply irresistible.

This book contains more than fifty classic and novel recipes for creating crispy, crunchy tortilla chips with tasty toppings. The recipes include simple and quick snacks, fancier appetizers, full-plate nachos that can be served as meals (including breakfast), party platters, and even a few dessert nachos. We cover the bottoms, middles, and tops—from frying chips at home to whipping up fresh salsas, grilled meats, and spicy toppers to cap off the well-dressed nacho. And because nachos don't require the skill level of a master chef, even people who consider microwave popcorn "cooking" will find these nacho recipes easily do-able.

Compared with other snacks, nachos endure. They're honest, unassuming finger food. Every year a new snack trend blasts across the media. We've seen the wraps craze, the sticks-and-skewers movement, the chips-and-dips approach, fondue flashes, and Martha Stewart manuals. But none of these possesses the same quick-and-easy, perennial, and down-to-earth appeal as nachos.

Nachos have been called "Mexican pizzas," and indeed they have much in common with the world's favorite food. As with pizzas, nachos can be adorned as plainly or as ambitiously as you like. But unlike pizzas, nachos are marvelously easy to make and lightning-quick to cook, qualities that only add to their charm. Their basic ingredients are everyone's favorites: corn chips, melted cheese, and spice, all without being too complicated or too stuffy to enjoy at a moment's notice.

As a kid in Texas, I grew up on Tex-Mex nachos, the kind topped solely with beans, cheese, and jalapeños. Gradually, my repertoire of nachos grew to include toppers like barbecue pork, fajitas, smoked chicken, grilled shrimp, and crisp vegetables. I expanded my nacho ingredients but retained an emphasis on Southwestern flavorings.

Then, in 1994, I launched the Web's first food and cooking e-zine, known as GlobalGourmet.com. My mission became (and still is) to bring my readers "the

WHAT MAKES NACHOS SO MACHO?

The nacho has universal appeal: It's a finger food, it crunches, it's cheesy, it's easy, it's tasty, quick, and satisfying. Anyone can make them. The nacho is as far from complicated and as close to irresistible as any snack can be.

- Nachos are all about instant gratification: Forget about threading little pieces of meat onto skewers, precise measuring, or the labor-intensive tasks common to other finger foods.
- Great-tasting nachos can be made with just two ingredients. Or upgrade your nacho by assembling more flavors and mixing up wild combinations, taking advantage of the handy variety of supermarket ready-to-use products, which range from shredded cheese to roasted peppers and smoked chicken in the deli case.
- Forget fancy equipment. A baking sheet and cheese grater will do.
- Nachos are decidedly more about eating than about cooking. They demand almost no kitchen skills. In fact, they don't require much of a kitchen at all. A cutting board and a toaster oven can work just fine.
- Homemade nachos need no advance preparation. They're ideal for spontaneous bursts of kitchen creativity and sudden snack attacks. Who has time to make pizza dough from scratch or plan ahead for it to rise? Nachos can be whipped up on the spot as a casual meal, and instantly perk up a party.

In short, nachos are the ideal fast food—cooked at home—but they're decidedly not junk food, not if they're made with wholesome, quality ingredients. You can whip up a robust tray of nachos in less time than it takes to blend a batch of margaritas, using simple ingredients that most families (and even kitchen-clueless bachelors) have on hand. Not many other finger foods can make the same claim—and still taste as satisfying and gratifying as homemade nachos do. And that's what makes nachos so macho.

world on a plate." So naturally, I started fiddling around with exotic nachos, giving the Tex-Mex dish a passport to worldly flavors and ethnic ingredients. I'm confident that no matter how wacky Chinese Firecracker Nachos (page 55) or Bombay Nachos with Curried Chickpeas and Tomato-Garlic Chutney (page 66) may sound, you'll devour them just as eagerly as you would a plate of traditional melted cheese and bean nachos, bubbling hot from the oven. Forget plates, I've happily discovered. Now we can have the world on a chip.

THE BASIC

NACHO FORMULA

It's not rocket science, but there are a few handy tips you should follow. . . .

EQUIPMENT AND TECHNIQUES

baking equipment

A heatproof baking sheet or platter is essential. Most recipes in this book are designed to fill a single layer in a 12 × 18-inch metal sheet pan, with low sides of about 1/2 inch—this is what I consider a "tray" of nachos. You can use other size pans or platters, as long as they can withstand high heat from the oven or broiler. You can also use smaller pans and cook the recipe in batches, or cook just half the recipe. Recipes that are more likely to be served in smaller quantities, such as the snazzy Caviar and Chive Nachos (page 62), are scaled to make just a half-tray of nachos. (For a full tray, double the ingredients in those recipes and cook in a single pan.)

nonstick materials

Melted cheese tastes so good that it's a shame to leave any stuck to the pan. And who wants to spend more time cleaning a pan than cooking in it? No one.

Nonstick pans are the best option if you have them, but if not . . .

Foil and Nonstick Spray

One option is to line a regular baking sheet with foil. A light spritz of nonstick vegetable spray on the foil prevents the cheese from sticking. Foil also makes for instant cleanup—just crumple and toss when done. You can also spritz pizza pans, pie pans, and disposable foil baking sheets.

Nonstick Foil

Better than regular foil is a product called Reynolds Wrap Release. It really works. Without being greasy, one side of the foil is magically treated to prevent food from sticking to it. Nachos lift right off, so you can easily transfer them to a separate serving platter if desired.

Parchment Paper or Nonstick Liners

Parchment paper and nonstick liners are other good options. Some nonstick liners are reusable and rinse clean instantly. Parchment paper, like foil, is entirely disposable and is naturally nonstick, so it doesn't need a spritz of nonstick spray. Use it once, then toss. Many supermarkets now sell parchment paper in rolls, and cookware stores stock reusable and other specialty liners.

Ovenproof Platters

If you plan to serve nachos for parties, you may want to invest in some attractive ovenproof platters. Ceramic ones work well, but make sure they're not glazed with lead (lead-glazed pieces are required to be labeled as such).

If you have a serving platter that's not ovenproof: Cook the nachos on a good nonstick surface, then transfer the nachos from the cooking pan to the serving platter. Gently lift or slide the nachos with a wide spatula onto the platter.

DON'T GET STUCK

The four best ways to keep melted cheese from sticking to your cooking surfaces are:

1. Use a nonstick pan
2. Line the pan with parchment paper or a reusable nonstick liner
3. Line the pan with nonstick aluminum foil, a special product called Reynolds Wrap Release
4. Line a regular pan with aluminum foil and spritz the foil with nonstick spray

recipe yields

A 12 × 18-inch pan or equivalent holds 4 to 5 ounces of tortilla chips in a single layer, or about 4 cups according to some cookbooks. I hope no one actually measures their chips by the cup—that's just too compulsive—and weighing the chips isn't totally accurate either, since thicker chips weigh more than thin ones. Suffice it to say that a 12 × 18-inch tray's worth of nachos feeds two people for lunch, four as a snack, and six if passed as an appetizer at a party.

NACHO LORE

Nachos were invented, as the most widely accepted legend goes, in 1943 at the Victory Club in Piedras Negras, across the Rio Grande River from Eagle Pass, Texas. A group of officers' wives on a shopping trip stopped in, and while gossiping and imbibing, asked for a snack. The chef, however, was not around, so the maître d' scurried to the kitchen, plunked some Wisconsin cheese on some fried tostadas, shoved them under the salamander (a restaurant broiler) until the cheese melted, then plopped some sliced jalapeños on top. The ladies loved them, calling them "Nacho's Especiales," in honor of their creator, Ignacio Anaya. "Nacho" is a nickname for "Ignacio."

Another version of the tale says that just one lady came in after hours when the main chef was gone. But she was from a wealthy, important family, so Ignacio, himself a chef, took to the kitchen and created nachos—with cheese, jalapeños, and another ingredient: refried beans.

In yet another version, a different restaurant, Crosby's, in Ciudad Acuña, across the border from Del Rio, Texas, claims to be the source of the original nacho. The same guy, Ignacio Anaya, created them, and in this story he was from Piedras Negras but worked at Crosby's. He developed his namesake snack for just a regular group of hungry folk, not a wealthy matron or a bunch of officers' wives.

For true nacho connoisseurs, 1975 was a black year. Not only did the original creator of nachos, Ignacio "Nacho" Anaya, pass away, but also in that same year, "nachos" debuted at a concession stand at the Texas Rangers Stadium in Arlington. But these weren't Nacho's nachos. They were, sadly, the progenitors of the gooey, gloppy orange mess now peddled nationwide as "nachos," and a favorite food of Homer Simpson.

cooking nachos

Some folks (with tongues bulging in cheeks) swear you can cook nachos in the heat of the Texas sun, but a kitchen and a hot oven or broiler work best.

Bake or broil, which is better? You can do either. The types of topper ingredients, the meltability of the cheese, and the thickness of the layers all affect the cooking method. In general, here's what I've found works well:

Broiling

If you broil too close to the heat source, the chips will burn before the cheese melts. If you set the rack about 7 inches below the broiler, you should be okay, but watch closely and check often to make sure the chips don't burn, especially around the edge of the pan (unless you like them that way). Always preheat the broiler, so the cheese starts melting as soon as the pan goes in. Broiling has its merits: It cooks nachos really quickly, without drying out the meats and other ingredients or causing them to release juices that can turn chips soggy.

Baking

Rule of thumb: Bake at 475°F. until the cheese is melted and starts to bubble. This usually takes about 5 minutes but can vary either way, depending on the amount and type of cheese. Be sure to preheat the oven until it comes to the right temperature. Overall, this method produces the most consistently perfect nachos, without much risk of burning too quickly. I set the oven rack 7 inches from the top of the oven, on the second rack, so the nachos cook in the hotter top third of the oven. And because my broiler is attached to the oven ceiling, I can switch from bake to broil and put a final bronzed tan on the nachos without adjusting the oven rack.

Other cookbooks recommend baking nachos at 350 to 450°F., rather than my preferred methods of baking at 475°F. or broiling about 7 inches from the heat source. In most cases, I've found that the lower heat settings generally don't work—the cheese dries out or the chips become soggy. But in some recipes, lower heat is necessary to cook the topping through completely, as in Crabmeat and Spinach Nachos (page 68).

THE MEXICAN DELI: ¡VAMONOS!

Mexican markets often have a hot deli section, which can be a nacho maniac's heaven. Right there, all in one place, are steamy hot beans, shredded pork carnitas, spit-roasted chicken, beefy carne asada, chunky guacamole, orange rice, and a trio or more of mild to hot salsas—all freshly made and just waiting to come home with you and jump on your nachos. Nachos don't require huge quantities of ingredients, so small containers (usually pints or less) are ample for whipping up a nacho party. Don't forget the freshly fried chips, Mexican cheeses, and tangy *cremas* (similar to crème fraîche or sour cream), and make sure to hit the produce section, packed with spicy chiles, sweet peppers, leafy cilantro, and crisp lettuces, while you're there.

Microwave Cheating

I'm not a fan of nachos cooked entirely in the microwave. They taste fake. The cheese tends to separate, leaving oily residue; the nachos never cook evenly; and they don't brown. Nachos should have a toastiness to them, which microwave ovens don't provide. However, I have been known to kick-start the cheese-melting process in a microwave, especially if the baked or broiled chips or other layers are likely to burn before the topping melts completely. Just layer the cheese on the chips in a pan that is both ovenproof and microwave-safe (such as a Pyrex pie pan or platter), and nuke them on high until the cheese *just* starts to soften but still has some solid shreds, about 30 to 60 seconds. After this brief microwave blast, add your other toppings. Then bake or broil until done. (I also jump-start grilled-cheese sandwiches in the microwave, then lightly toast them in a skillet. This prevents the all-too-common "charcoal cheese sandwich" syndrome.)

BOTTOMS: FRIED, FLAVORED, AND BAKED

The secret is in the chip. Unlike pizza, whose dough is benign enough to support almost any flavor, nachos typically burst with hearty corn flavor and toothsome crunch. Of course you can pick up poufy bags of standard corn chips at the corner mini-mart or neighborhood supermarket; these chips off the ol' block can be tasty and are certainly convenient. But to put more macho in your nacho, seek out other chip varieties, like these:

home-fried corn chips

Freshly fried tortilla chips made at home, hot out of the oil, taste so good they're usually consumed before you can say *¡Vamonos!* If self-control is a problem, or if you prefer more convenience, pick up freshly cooked chips from several sources: Mexican markets with hot food sections often fry their own chips, as do tortillarias. Better-quality Mexican restaurants also cook their own chips daily. Ask to buy a bag, which are usually as cheap as store-bought but more convenient than frying chips at home. If you're throwing a party, these freshly fried chips can put the icing on the cake (or the cheese on the chip, so to speak).

FRESHLY FRIED CORN CHIPS

Stale corn tortillas produce crisper chips than fresh tortillas. For nachos, slice the tortillas into 4 or 6 wedges. If the tortillas are very fresh, leave the wedges out at room temperature for one hour before frying.

First, you need a heavy, deep pot (or use a deep-fat fryer and follow the manufacturer's instructions for oil depth and heating). Fill the pot with 2 to 3 inches of corn, canola, or vegetable oil. Heat the oil over medium-high flame until a deep-frying thermometer registers between 365°F. and 375°F. If you don't have such a thermometer, test the temperature by dropping a chip into the oil. If the oil bubbles instantly and the chip rises to the surface, it's ready.

Carefully drop in only a handful of chips at a time, so the oil stays at optimum temperature. Stir them around with a strainer or slotted spoon to separate them. When the chips are light brown, in 1 or 2 minutes, scoop them out with the strainer, letting excess oil drip back into the pot, and dump them out on paper towels to drain. Salt the chips as desired. Continue frying remaining chips in batches until done.

flavored chips

Corn chips aren't just yellow or white. Chips with added natural flavors and ingredients can be quite colorful and festive. Consider these varieties:

- Orange: chipotle-flavored
- Green: avocado-flavored, such as El Sabroso Guaca Chips
- Blue: The ones that include sesame seeds are especially good for Asian toppings
- Bean: from pinto or black beans

Even plain corn chips can range from nearly white to pale yellow to deep gold. And don't forget the infinite variety of chips dusted with flavors, like Ranch, Salsa,

Lime, "Nacho"-flavored chips, and other grocery-aisle favorites. But beware: Some chips are too salty to make a good nacho, especially if your toppings are also on the salty side, as with ham, feta cheese, or olives. With salty toppers, opt for low-salt or no-salt chips.

shape, texture, and thickness

Does the manner in which a chip is formed make a difference? Yep, but it depends on the nacho. Sometimes you want a sturdy chip to support a tower of ingredients without breaking. But with fewer ingredients or more refined ones, a thinner, subtler chip works best.

For instance, the Caviar and Chive Nachos (page 62) and the Lox and Cream Cheese Nachos (page 88) in this book require a delicate chip, one with a mild corn flavor, just a touch of salt, and a smoother texture than that of the typical corn chip. I found just the right product in Torengos: These ultra-thin, crisp chips are the Pringles of the corn chip aisle; they're pressed and formed like a bakery product, shaped into perfect, identical triangles. Toppings neatly and pristinely nestle in their bowl-like, slightly concave shape. Arranged on a tray, they make an elegant presentation for a black-tie affair, and they come stacked in a can, so there are no broken fragments to contend with.

But sometimes, as with a hearty bean-and-cheese nacho, a thick, rustic chip supports the weight of the toppings better than a thinner chip. The shape of the chip usually doesn't make as much difference as the thickness, so circles and triangles can pretty

OVEN-BAKED ALTERNATIVES

The basic formula for baked chips, whether they're made from pita bread, whole-wheat flour tortillas, or standard white flour tortillas, is the same.

1. Heat the oven to 375°F. with an oven rack in the center position.

2. Spritz a flour tortilla lightly with nonstick spray, then slice into 4, 6, or 8 wedges. Arrange the wedges on a baking sheet. If using pita bread, split the top and bottom rounds apart first, then slice each round into wedges. (A pizza cutter does a fine job of wedge-cutting, or use a sharp knife.)

3. Bake for 5 to 10 minutes, or until the wedges crisp up and turn toasty. Let cool slightly before using.

Note: If you're using a light topping, as with the dessert nachos in this book, you don't need to precrisp the raw wedges into chips before adding toppings.

much be used interchangeably. Fried tortilla strips are less desirable, unless you're strewing them across the tray and don't care about picking up each nacho chip separately.

flour tortilla and other alternative chips

Corn chips, with their assertive corn flavor, don't always taste best with all ingredients. Dessert nachos in particular do well with the milder taste of flour tortilla chips. I don't know of anyone who sells commercially baked flour tortilla chips, but you can crisp them up at home in minutes (see Oven-Baked Alternatives on page 19).

(see Oven-Baked Alternatives on page 19)

Home-baked chips from whole-wheat flour tortillas and pita bread lend themselves well to Middle Eastern ingredients. Chip makers are coming up with new types of snacks daily, so experiment. Some of these products (such as the delicate wheat-flavored Sun Chips) can put a unique spin on traditional nachos.

Finally, some corn chips are baked rather than fried. They're not my first choice, simply because I'm nuts for fried chips. But there's nothing wrong with using baked corn chips if that's what you prefer.

CHEESES: MELTERS, SOFTIES, CRUMBLES, AND DUSTERS

The French (from a country the size of Texas) boast that they could serve a different type of cheese every day for a year, perhaps two years. Their fierce nationalistic pride about cheese is certainly justified, and they would probably utter *"Sacrebleu!"* to see a majestic, monastery cheese such as Pont l'Évêque or a delicately nutty Gruyère de Comté adorn a nacho. But don't let that stop you from going whole hog, so to speak.

It goes without saying that the tastier the ingredient, including the cheese, the tastier the nacho. But nachos don't need expensive imported cheeses to taste good. Common, everyday cheeses do just fine as nacho toppers.

The average North American supermarket stocks about thirty types of cheese, only a handful of which are imported. Yet, these days, the domestic cheeses in our supermarkets and whole-food markets can be of remarkably good quality, and many American aged and artisanal cheeses give some mighty stiff competition to the European imports. At the same time, if you're hankering for a world-class touch, specialty cheeses from Spain, Italy, Switzerland, Mexico, Britain, and, of course, France can dramatically transform the everyday nacho snack into a four-star appetizer.

When it comes to convenience, supermarket cheeses rule. Packages of preshredded and sliced cheeses make nacho assembly a snap. Cheddar, Monterey Jack, mozzarella, Parmesan, and some Mexican and Italian cheese blends (which combine two, three, or sometimes up to six types of compatible cheeses) are the most commonly sold shredded cheeses. Swiss, provolone, and Muenster come handily sliced: Just tear them up into pieces and layer them on the chips, and they melt as well as the shredded cheeses.

Chunks of cheese should be grated or shredded using a hand grater or a food processor. Grating may be an extra preparation step, but it opens the door to a wider variety of cheeses. Ethnic delis and gourmet shops offer the nacho cook a vast array of exotic options, but you won't find these full-flavored delicacies preshredded. To enjoy them, you'll simply have to do that yourself. Some of my favorites are Spanish sheep's milk manchego (different from Mexican manchego); Italian fontina; Mexican asadero; British farmhouse Cheshire; Dutch goat Gouda; Swiss Appenzeller; artisanal sheep, goat, and cow milk cheeses hailing from California to Vermont; and French Gruyère de Comté, one of the finest Swiss-style cheeses.

No matter where they were made, the best nacho cheeses can be divided into four main categories, based on their melting abilities. You can top a nacho with a single cheese, or combine different types of cheeses with contrasting textures and flavors.

melters

These firm cheeses melt smoothly and easily. Pile them on as the main flavor base, or sprinkle a light layer over the chip as a barrier against moister ingredients (like meats or veggies), which may turn the chip soggy. Examples: cheddar, Monterey Jack, Gouda, Muenster, Swiss, mozzarella.

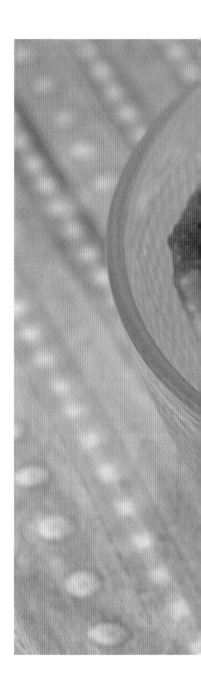

A NON-SURFER'S GUIDE TO SHREDDING AND RIPPING

How can a single ounce of cheese, when shredded, measure as little as ⅓ cup in some cases and more than 1 whole cup in others? The equipment used to shred the cheese produces dramatically different results. *Gourmet* (February 2003) subjected an ounce of cheese to a hand grater, rotary grater, box grater, a Microplane rasp, and a food processor. The smallest volume came from the food processor, as ⅓ cup of fine pebbles. The largest consisted of a whopping 1¼ cups of feathery wisps planed off the rasp. Most other methods hovered around ½ cup of shredded cheese. The cheese texture, I've found, also makes a difference. An ounce of a hard cheese like Parmesan will fill less volume than the same weight of a moister cheese, like Monterey Jack. In the recipes that follow, I've specified both the weight and approximate volume of shredded cheeses. Sliced cheeses, which you merely rip into pieces to layer on nachos, are listed by weight only. Fortunately, nachos are very forgiving. Weight is the more accurate measure, but if you find weighing the cheese on a scale too bothersome, simply use the quantity that seems to work best for you.

SPICE AND HERB SPRINKLES

Enhance a nacho simply by sprinkling on fresh or dried herbs and spices. Winning combinations:

- Caraway seeds with Muenster
- Toasted cumin seeds with pepper Jack
- White pepper or thyme with Swiss, Emmentaler, or Gruyère
- Curry powder with cheddar
- Black pepper with any cheese

softies

These spreadable cheeses are soft or pillowy, adding a mouthful of contrast against the crisp chip. Simply spread, spoon, or pipe them on. They may be added to a nacho before or after cooking, but if they're extremely moist or buttery (such as Gorgonzola), it's generally best to add them after cooking. These cheeses are often sold flavored with herbs and spices. Examples: Boursin, cream cheese, Neufchâtel, blue cheeses, cheese spreads.

crumbles

As the name suggests, these cheeses can be crumbled on by hand. Crumbles are not as moist as Softies, which are more spreadable, yet they're not as dry and hard as Dusters, which must be grated. They're usually characterized by sharp, intense, and sometimes salty flavors, making them good accents to other very potent toppings. Examples: feta, queso fresco, fresh goat cheeses.

dusters

Hard cheeses can be a bit salty, but only a small amount, finely grated, is needed to zing up a nacho. I usually sprinkle them on as a final topping to nachos baked with a lower layer of Melters or Softies. Examples: Parmesan, Romano, dry Jack, ricotta salata.

The cheese you pick is the most critical element of a nacho. Depending on the other toppings, you may want a slightly sweet and nutty cheese from the Swiss family, a mild mozzarella, or an intensely sharp blue-veined Stilton. Some of the most distinctive nachos are made with sheep and goat milk cheeses or aged cheeses, like aged cheddar. Smoked cheeses are intensely potent.

While a robust, in-your-face, strong cheesy taste may sound appealing, too much of a good thing can sometimes be overpowering. So don't be shy about mixing and matching cheeses on a nacho to create just the right balance of flavor and texture. To test a flavor mix, microwave a single chip with your choices on it, just to see how

Continued on page 28

CHILE DICIN' IN D.C.

Whenever Texans land in Washington, they seem to turn the whole town upside down. Before the Bush family took residence, the White House had already sampled its fair share of nachos, chili con queso, and chalupas, courtesy of Lyndon Johnson's administration. When Lyndon, Lady Bird, and family rolled into 1600 Pennsylvania Avenue, either the prospect of preparing Tex-Mex vittles for the new first family was too gauche for the extremely French White House chef who'd been installed by Jackie Kennedy, or the panorama of daily haute cuisine was too stuffy for the Johnsons. For whatever reason, a new White House executive chef, a Swiss named Henry Haller, was brought in.

With true Texas pride, the Johnson family served their beloved Tex-Mex specialties to heads of state, dignitaries, politicians, and at special events. A flexible cook, Chef Haller eagerly replicated his new boss's down-home dishes authentically, including making chile con queso with cans of Ro*Tel Tomatoes and Green Chiles (a Texas tradition) and using real American cheese (not cheddar). Describing the president's first annual congressional reception, *CBS Evening News* anchor Eric Sevareid acknowledged that Haller's "chili with cheese last night was reported by survivors as first class."

The chef's jalapeño-capped nacho recipe even appears in his book, *The White House Family Cookbook*. "Steaming nachos adorned a long buffet table decorated with yellow flowers," he writes, describing Luci Johnson's bridesmaid party, while miniature chalupas were the cheery centerpiece for Lynda's bridesmaid affair. Chef Haller's Tex-Mex dishes earned him more than braggin' rights. He remained White House chef for twenty-two years, serving everything from nachos to lobster Newburg, for the Johnson, Nixon, Ford, Carter, and Reagan administrations.

Smoked Chicken, Roasted Peppers, and Asiago Nachos, page 36

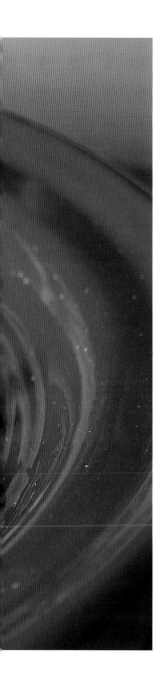

YANKEE NACHOS

What constitutes the quintessential nacho? *Cook's Illustrated,* an excellent magazine known as "America's test-kitchen," published in Massachusetts, came up with what some Texans would consider "Yankee nachos." In a nutshell, they said to bake nachos at 400°F. for 7 to 10 minutes, using a double layer of chips and cheese in a 13 × 9-inch baking dish, and finish with a sprinkling of chiles. Around the edges of the pan, after the nachos are cooked, drop scoops of sour cream, guacamole, and salsa (without them, nachos look "buck naked," according to the article). Pass lime wedges separately. *Cook's Illustrated* says their nachos aren't "fancy French cuisine or exotic ethnic fare. This is simple American junk food, done right."

I'm not sure their version would pass in the White House as American nachos "done right"—at least not since Johnson and Bush saddled up the presidential cowboy seat. But even Texans can differ on how nachos are best made. Here's what a true Texan (you know it when you hear her speak), Paula Lambert, president of the Mozzarella Company in Dallas, has to say:

"I don't think the recipe in *Cook's Illustrated* is quite authentic. They must all be Yankees, and they just don't know what a real Tex-Mex nacho is. The best nachos are at Joe T. Garcia's in Fort Worth. They are whole, round corn tortillas that are first fried and then placed under the broiler or in a very hot oven, topped with longhorn cheese, and then topped only with canned sliced jalapeños. They're toasted until they begin to brown on the edges, but no longer. There are many other versions—like the one with refried beans under the longhorn cheese—that are good, but none surpass Joe Garcia's. The worst nachos are found in ballparks and discount department stores where they put a mound of corn chips in a little paper dish, pour processed liquid cheese on top, and then top that with chopped jalapeños. Ugh!"

For another type of authentic Tex-Mex nacho—the kind with cheese, chiles, and beans—flip to the recipe for Traditional Tex-Mex "Nacho's Nachos" (page 32).

- Select thicker chips for dense or moist toppers
- Precook meats and certain veggies to remove moisture (even a zap in a microwave can help release moisture)
- Use small pieces (diced, chopped, minced, ground)
- Choose raw veggies that won't weep, or drain those that do (such as tomatoes)
- Wait until after baking to garnish with greens or sprouts

the combination tastes. Then bake or broil a full tray once you've hit on the right combination.

When it comes to nacho fixin', forget about ethnic origins and family bloodlines. Nachos are the United Nations of the snack world, not the Royal Family. Muenster cheese may have roots in France and Germany, but this mild melter balances the spicy-sweet Chinese pork in Chinese Firecracker Nachos (page 55) perfectly, and its soft texture helps hold the other toppings in place. A Greek cheese and an East Indian curry may seem an unlikely combination, but the salty sharpness of feta zips up both the flavor and color of the warmly spiced Bombay Nachos with Curried Chickpeas and Tomato-Garlic Chutney (page 66). Even simple Italian BLT Nachos (page 35) profit from a bubbly layer of tangy provolone and Italian seasonings.

TOPPERS: MEATS, FISH, FOWL, BEANS, AND VEGGIES

Nachos can be made, start to finish, in ten minutes with ready-to-use ingredients. Or you can spend an extra fifteen minutes or so to whip up some custom-cooked additions. Just about anything goes, but you do want to pay attention to two aspects: salt and moisture.

Processed foods, such as sliced deli meats, olives, pickles, and sausages, get much of their characteristic flavor from salt. When adding them to nachos, take care that once combined, the chips, cheese, and toppers don't create a salt explosion. Using unsalted or less salty chips can help, and stay away from inherently salty cheeses like feta if the other toppers are salty.

No soggy bottoms. *No soggy bottoms.* It's like a mantra. Soggy chips come from toppers (typically refried beans, sauces, or vegetables) that are either too moist to begin with or too thickly spread on the chip. A light smear of refried beans is all that's needed for flavor, and it won't bog down the chip. Also, a thin layer of cheese between the chip and the sauce will act as a moisture barrier. And, of course, a thick chip is better suited to moist ingredients than a thin chip.

You don't have to layer on all the ingredients before cooking the nachos either. Assemble the nachos with only those ingredients that you prefer melted or heated. Caviar, smoked salmon, shredded lettuce and cabbage, fresh chopped parsley and cilantro—these are the types of ingredients to toss on *after* the nachos are cooked.

Along with cheeses, salsas, and streakers (see pages 70 to 85), the main categories of nacho toppers include the following:

off-the-shelf, deli-ready, or prepared foods

Sliced or chunked deli meats, smoked salmon and lox, rotisserie chicken, cooked bacon, cooked sausage, prepared barbecue brisket, prepared taco meat, carnitas, chile con carne, cooked bacon bits, cooked seafood (shrimp, crab, lobster, tuna), canned beans and Mexican take-out beans, sun-dried tomatoes, pesto, pickled jalapeños, pepperoncini, bottled roasted sweet and hot peppers, enchilada sauce, hummus, olives, artichoke hearts, frozen or canned corn, and fruit spreads for dessert nachos.

fresh raw ingredients

Onions, garlic, tomatoes, lettuce, peppers, chiles, jicama, cilantro and other fresh herbs, mushrooms, spinach, cabbage and napa cabbage, mango, pineapple, avocado, sprouts.

custom-cooked ingredients

Anything you make at home qualifies, including leftovers. This book includes quick-to-fix recipes for Chinese Firecracker Nachos (page 55), Jamaican Rum Chicken Nachos with Ginger-Watermelon Salsa (page 50), Charred Corn, Chicken, and Avocado Crema Nachos (page 58), and more.

SPEEDY

Traditional Tex-Mex "Nacho's Nachos"

BBQ Chicken and Smoked Cheese Nachos

Italian BLT Nachos

Smoked Chicken, Roasted Peppers, and Asiago Nachos

Arroz con QUESO Nachos

Make these nachos in a Texas-lightning flash, solely with ready-to-use or raw ingredients. Round up your resources in the supermarket or Mexican deli, canned and frozen-food aisles, and the fresh-produce section. Seek out quality time-savers like gourmet sausages, cooked taco meat, and barbecued brisket, then trot out to the table hot trays of your own original nachos.

NACHOS

HAWAIIAN Pineapple and Canadian BACON Nachos

Portuguese **Pizza** Nachos

Nachos de Carnitas

Spicy Thai Beef Nachos with PEANUT Sauce

Frico "Nachitos"

TRADITIONAL **TEX-MEX**
"NACHO'S NACHOS"

makes one 12 × 18-inch tray or equivalent

One legend has it that the original nacho, as invented by Ignacio "Nacho" Anaya, was topped only with cheese and jalapeños. Refried beans came later. Another tale includes refried beans as part of the original nacho. Regardless of whether "refritos" were or were not part of Nacho's first nacho, they were part of the first nachos *I* ever tasted and have always represented true Tex-Mex nachos to me. The softness of the beans against the delicate crunch of the chip, topped with hot, melted cheese and a spicy jalapeño, gives these nachos their unique character. Some folks prefer to use fresh jalapeños, but I like the vinegary pucker that comes from pickled ones ("en escabeche").

• see photo on page 34 •

4 to 5 ounces corn tortilla chips
1 to 1½ cups refried beans

6 to 8 ounces shredded cheddar (1½ to 2 cups)
2 to 3 pickled jalapeños, sliced

1. Preheat the oven to 475°F., or preheat the broiler, with the rack positioned about 7 inches from the top of the oven or the heat source.

2. Assemble the nachos: For thin chips, use less of each each topping; for thick chips, use more. Smear each tortilla chip with a dab of beans and arrange in a single layer on a 12 × 18-inch baking sheet or ovenproof platter. Sprinkle the cheese evenly over the top. Place a jalapeño slice on each chip.

3. Bake the nachos for 4 to 6 minutes, or broil, until the cheese is melted and bubbly.

variation: seasoned nachos I can't call this version authentic, but it tastes good anyway: After adding the cheese, sprinkle on ½ teaspoon toasted cumin seeds and ¼ teaspoon ground red chile, followed by the jalapeños. Top with ½ cup diced red, yellow, or green onion, and cook as above.

BBQ CHICKEN AND SMOKED CHEESE NACHOS

makes one 12 × 18-inch tray or equivalent

If you're a fan of barbecue chicken pizza, you'll want a whole tray of these nachos just for yourself. You can cook the Barbecued Chicken (page 73) from scratch or buy precooked chicken breast meat from the supermarket.

8 to 10 ounces cooked chicken breast meat, such as Barbecued Chicken (page 73) or store-bought, about 2 small to medium breast halves, diced

2 tablespoons prepared barbecue sauce

4 to 5 ounces corn tortilla chips

3 ounces shredded Cappiello (smoked braided mozzarella) or other smoked mozzarella (about 1 cup)

3 ounces shredded Monterey Jack (about 1 cup)

1/2 cup diced red onion

1/4 cup chopped fresh cilantro

1 recipe Lemon-Pepper Cole Slaw (page 84) (optional)

1. Preheat the oven to 475°F., or preheat the broiler, with the rack positioned about 7 inches from the top of the oven or the heat source.

2. In a small bowl, toss the diced chicken with the barbecue sauce until well coated.

3. Assemble the nachos: For thin chips, use less of each topping; for thick chips, use more. Arrange the chips in a single layer on a 12 × 18-inch baking sheet or ovenproof platter. Sprinkle both cheeses evenly over the chips. Spoon some barbecued chicken and red onion onto each chip.

4. Bake the nachos for 4 to 6 minutes, or broil, until the cheese is melted and bubbly.

5. Lightly toss on the chopped cilantro and Lemon-Pepper Cole Slaw, if using, and serve.

ABOVE: ITALIAN BLT NACHOS, right • below: traditional tex-mex "nacho's nachos," page 32

34

ITALIAN **BLT** NACHOS

makes one 12 × 18-inch tray or equivalent

Color me happy the day I discovered bags of cooked, real crumbled bacon (not the fake bacon bits) in the supermarket. What carnivorous cook doesn't appreciate bacon that is already fried (no mess!) and ready to toss into salads, or in this case, on nachos? A one-pound bag made by Hormel sells for about five dollars at warehouse stores. Use what you need and refrigerate the rest.

Here's my favorite BLT sandwich: toasted sourdough bread, slathered with mayonnaise, sprinkled with Italian seasoning (a dried herb mix), a pinch of granulated garlic, fresh ground pepper, sliced provolone cheese, crispy bacon, ripe tomato, and red or oak leaf lettuce. I make nachos the same way, substituting corn chips for the sourdough. The precooked, crumbled bacon makes the nachos easier and quicker to prepare than a sandwich, and the chips, of course, add a most satisfying crunch.

Note: You may make the Italian-Seasoned Mayonnaise (page 84) a day in advance; store refrigerated until ready to use. Instead of diced whole tomatoes, 5 ounces of small grape or cherry tomatoes may be halved or quartered and placed on individual nachos.

4 to 5 ounces corn tortilla chips

6 to 8 ounces provolone, shredded (about 2 cups) or sliced

3/4 cup crumbled cooked bacon pieces (about 2 1/2 ounces)

1 cup finely shredded lettuce

2 Roma tomatoes, chopped (about 1 heaping cup)

1 recipe Italian-Seasoned Mayonnaise (page 84)

1. Preheat the oven to 475°F., or preheat the broiler, with the rack positioned about 7 inches from the top of the oven or the heat source.

2. Assemble the nachos: Arrange the chips in a single layer on a 12 × 18-inch baking sheet or ovenproof platter. Sprinkle the cheese evenly over the top (if using sliced cheese, tear or cut it into pieces and cover chips evenly). Sprinkle on the bacon.

3. Bake the nachos for 4 to 6 minutes, or broil, until the cheese is melted and bubbly.

4. Sprinkle the lettuce over the nachos, spoon on the chopped tomato, then drizzle or splatter on the mayonnaise, making sure to get a bit of it on each nacho.

SMOKED CHICKEN, ROASTED PEPPERS, AND ASIAGO NACHOS

makes one 12 × 18-inch tray or equivalent

Next time you smoke or grill chicken, save or freeze some pieces for nachos. Smoked chicken also comes in packages in supermarkets, or you can dice up a rotisserie chicken from the hot deli case. Roasted red and yellow peppers are handy for all sorts of uses, from nachos like these to pastas and salads. Cook them from scratch (page 80) or pick up a jar of roasted peppers at an Italian deli or specialty market. The mellow sharpness of Asiago cheese punctuates the smokiness of the peppers and chicken perfectly. But Asiago is a bit on the dry side as cheeses go, so be careful not to overcook these nachos. For a creamier topping, replace one-third of the Asiago with Monterey Jack.

4 to 5 ounces corn tortilla chips
10 ounces shredded Asiago (about 3 cups)
1 cup packed, diced, smoked chicken meat
  (about 1 half-breast, or 6 ounces)

1 cup diced or slivered roasted red and yellow sweet peppers (about 7 ounces), bottled or from scratch (page 80)
Freshly ground black pepper to taste

1. Preheat the oven to 475°F., or preheat the broiler, with the rack positioned about 7 inches from the top of the oven or the heat source.

2. Assemble the nachos: Arrange the chips on a 12 × 18-inch baking sheet or ovenproof platter. Sprinkle on half the cheese, then top with the chicken, the remaining cheese, and the peppers. Grind fresh black pepper on top.

3. Bake the nachos for 5 to 7 minutes, or broil, until the cheese is melted and bubbly.

ARROZ CON QUESO NACHOS

makes one 12 × 18-inch tray or equivalent

I have a favorite way of enjoying the Mexican-style rice that typically comes on combo platters—or is sold in pints or quarts at Mexican delis and supermarkets. I heat the rice with grated sharp cheddar cheese, then scoop it up with tortilla chips, sometimes adding a dash of green or red hot sauce. The contrast of the crunchy chip, the soft and tangy rice, and the buttery, sharp cheese is immensely satisfying, as much a comfort food as macaroni and cheese. I prefer to use the thick, sturdy tortilla chips found in Mexican delis for this hearty nacho.

4 to 5 ounces sturdy tortilla chips

6 to 8 ounces shredded sharp cheddar (about 2 cups)

8 ounces cooked Mexican rice (about 2¹/₂ cups)

Chile powder or finely chopped jalapeño to taste

Prepared or homemade salsa (optional)

1. Preheat the oven to 475°F., or preheat the broiler, with the rack positioned about 7 inches from the top of the oven or the heat source.

2. Assemble the nachos: Arrange the chips on a 12 × 18-inch baking sheet or oven-proof platter. Sprinkle the chips with half the cheese (as it melts, it will help hold the rice in place). Sprinkle on the rice, and top with the remaining cheese. Dust with a dash of chile powder or jalapeño (or both, if you're feeling *muy macho*).

3. Bake the nachos for 5 to 7 minutes, or broil, until the cheese is melted and bubbly.

4. Serve with salsa on the side, if desired.

HAWAIIAN PINEAPPLE AND CANADIAN BACON NACHOS

makes one 12 × 18-inch tray or equivalent

One of the seemingly oddest yet most popular pizzas combines Canadian bacon and pineapple. Actually, the flavor mix isn't that unusual—it's almost the same combination as Chinese sweet-and-sour pork. Plate up these Hawaiian Nachos with the Chinese Firecracker Nachos (page 55) as appetizers and you've got an exotic pupu platter (tiny paper parasols and flaming volcano are optional).

Note: Sun-dried tomato pesto is made from finely chopped sun-dried tomatoes packed in oil, and comes in jars in the produce section.

4 ounces sliced Canadian bacon (about 8 round slices)

4 ounces crumbled soft chèvre (goat cheese) (about 2/3 cup)

4 ounces shredded mozzarella (about 1½ cups)

4 ounces canned or fresh pineapple chunks

4 to 5 ounces corn tortilla chips

½ cup sun-dried tomato pesto

Crushed red pepper flakes to taste

1. Preheat the oven to 475°F., or preheat the broiler, with the rack positioned about 7 inches from the top of the oven or the heat source.

2. As if cutting a pizza, slice the Canadian bacon into wedges slightly smaller than the size of the chips. In a small bowl, loosely mix together the chèvre and mozzarella. If the pineapple chunks are large, cut them so they're about half the size of the Canadian bacon pieces.

3. Assemble the nachos: Arrange the chips in a single layer on a 12 × 18-inch baking sheet or ovenproof platter. Spoon or smear small amounts of the sun-dried tomato pesto over the chips. Sprinkle the cheeses evenly on top. Layer on the Canadian bacon, followed by the pineapple chunks. Sprinkle with the red pepper flakes.

4. Bake the nachos for 4 to 6 minutes, or broil, until the cheese is melted and bubbly.

ABOVE: HAWAIIAN PINEAPPLE AND CANADIAN BACON NACHOS, left • below: portuguese pizza nachos, page 40

PORTUGUESE PIZZA NACHOS

makes one 12 × 18-inch tray or equivalent

Fast and fabulous—and with only five ingredients! Linguiça, a Portuguese staple, is a mildly spicy smoked sausage made with pork shoulder, paprika, garlic, wine vinegar, and herbs. Look for it in supermarket meat sections, with a label that indicates "Fully Cooked." In California, I buy Silva brand. Slice it thin for a nacho topping, and use any leftover linguiça for soups, stews, potatoes, or eggs. The name is a variation of *lingua* or "tongue," a reference to its long, slender shape (it does not contain tongue as an ingredient).

Note: You can substitute pepperoni for linguiça in this recipe, but it's not the same. Linguiça has a much more complex, robust flavor and is less salty. Andouille and Polish sausages are other alternatives. The Mediterranean-spiced Sonoma Jack cheese adds its own distinctive layer of flavor, but you can also use regular Monterey Jack, pepper Jack, or your other favorite cheese here.

• see photo on page 39 •

1/4 cup coarsely chopped fresh cilantro
1/2 cup chopped marinated artichoke hearts
4 to 5 ounces corn tortilla chips

8 to 10 ounces shredded Mediterranean-spiced Sonoma Jack (about 3 cups)
6 to 8 ounces fully cooked linguiça sausage, thinly sliced

1. Preheat the oven to 475°F., or preheat the broiler, with the rack positioned about 7 inches from the top of the oven or the heat source.

2. Combine the cilantro and artichoke hearts in a small bowl.

3. Assemble the nachos: Arrange the chips on a 12 × 18-inch baking sheet or oven-proof platter. Sprinkle on the cheese, then top with the linguiça.

4. Bake the nachos for 5 to 7 minutes, or broil, until the cheese is melted and bubbly.

5. Spoon the cilantro-artichoke mixture on the nachos before serving.

NACHOS DE CARNITAS

makes one 12 × 18-inch tray or equivalent

Carnitas—meltingly soft pork chunks with crispy edges—are typically chopped into little bits and folded into steamy corn tortillas, then topped with salsa or Pico de Gallo (page 77) and lettuce. Absolute heaven! Mexican markets with hot deli counters sell cooked chunks of carnitas by the pound (along with fresh salsas and guacamole), which makes these nachos a snap to assemble.

4 to 5 ounces sturdy tortilla chips
1 pound cooked carnitas, coarsely chopped
3/4 teaspoon ground cumin
1/2 teaspoon granulated garlic
1/2 teaspoon finely ground black pepper
1/4 teaspoon salt, or to taste

8 to 10 ounces shredded Colby-Jack cheese (about 3 cups)
2 green onions, finely chopped (white and green parts)
Pico de Gallo (page 77) or salsa to taste
Chopped cilantro and finely julienned lettuce (optional)

1. Preheat the oven to 475°F., or preheat the broiler, with the rack positioned about 7 inches from the top of the oven or the heat source.

2. Assemble the nachos: Arrange the chips on a 12 × 18-inch baking sheet or oven-proof platter. In a separate bowl, toss the carnitas with the cumin, garlic, pepper, and salt. Sprinkle the cheese on the nachos, then top with the carnitas mixture and green onion.

3. Bake the nachos for 5 to 7 minutes, or broil, until the cheese is melted and bubbly.

4. Just before serving, lightly spoon on Pico de Gallo or salsa, and sprinkle with cilantro and lettuce, if desired.

ABOVE: SPICY THAI BEEF NACHOS WITH PEANUT SAUCE, right • below: frico "nachitos," page 44

SPICY THAI BEEF NACHOS WITH PEANUT SAUCE

makes one 12 × 18-inch tray or equivalent

Even in my local, rural supermarket, I can find authentic Asian products and sauces, so urban dwellers and country folk alike should have no problem picking up the ingredients for this speedy, spicy, Thai-inspired nacho. The brands in your area may be different (I use Thai Kitchen Red Curry Paste and Dynasty Thai Peanut Satay Sauce), but the same basic products are stocked in any Asian aisle.

Note: You may substitute deli-sliced chicken or turkey for the beef.

½ teaspoon Thai red curry paste, or to taste
4 ounces crumbled soft chèvre (goat cheese) (about ⅔ cup)
2 tablespoons Thai peanut satay sauce
2 teaspoons fresh lime juice

4 to 5 ounces corn tortilla chips
4 ounces shredded mozzarella (about 1½ cups)
6 ounces thinly sliced roast beef
½ cup coarsely chopped cilantro

1. Preheat the oven to 475°F., or preheat the broiler, with the rack positioned about 7 inches from the top of the oven or the heat source.

2. Mash together the curry paste and chèvre in a small bowl. In a separate small bowl, mix together the satay sauce and lime juice.

3. Assemble the nachos: Arrange the chips in a single layer on a 12 × 18-inch baking sheet or ovenproof platter. Sprinkle the mozzarella evenly over the chips. With your fingers, shred the roast beef into bite-size pieces and distribute over the cheese. On top of the roast beef, drop small bits of the chèvre mixture (use your fingers or two teaspoons).

4. Bake the nachos for 4 to 6 minutes, or broil, until the cheese is melted.

5. Drizzle the satay mixture over the nachos with a spoon. Toss on the cilantro and serve.

FRICO "NACHITOS"

makes two 8-inch nachitos, or 8 nachito quarters

You know the crusty cheese layer that forms in the bottom of a fondue pot? Arguably, it's the best part of the meal. Or have you ever tried the crispy, lacy rounds of fried cheese known in Italy as frico, or Friulian cheese crisps? I call this variation of the fried-cheese concept "nachitos"—crisp nacho-like treats cooked on top of the stove. It's also a tasty way to use up those tiny shards of crumbled chips at the bottom of the bag. If desired, you can garnish this with such goodies as sour cream and smoked salmon, salsa, or dips.

• see photo on page 42 •

2 ounces coarsely shredded Parmesan (about 1 cup lightly packed)

1 finely diced fresh jalapeño or serrano chile

4 tablespoons crushed corn chips

1. Warm an 8-inch nonstick skillet (or a regular skillet spritzed with nonstick spray) over medium heat.

2. For each nachito: Sprinkle a thin layer of grated cheese in the bottom of the pan, using about ¼ cup. On top of the cheese, sprinkle half the diced chiles. Crumble half the broken chips on top in a layer, then finish with another ¼ cup cheese. Press down gently on the mixture with a spatula, so the chips sink into the bottom layer of cheese.

3. Cook over medium-high heat until the cheese melts and starts to brown and crisp up on the bottom and edges; this will take 2 to 4 minutes. Use the spatula to gently lift the edges from the pan, then gently push the spatula under the center part to loosen it. Lift up and set the nachito on a plate or cutting board. Repeat with the remaining ingredients to make a second nachito.

4. Serve whole, letting people break off pieces to nibble on, or cut into wedges. Serve warm or at room temperature.

variations Heat a few drops of truffle oil, walnut oil, or other flavored oil in the pan before adding the cheese. Sprinkle in paprika, granulated garlic, chives, green onions, or herbs as the cheese melts. Try other cheeses, like Asiago, Gruyère, and cheddar.

BORDER NACHO LOVE: ANOTHER TEXAN'S PERSPECTIVE ON THE PERFECT NACHO

By W. Park Kerr, founder of El Paso Chile Company and distiller of Tequila Nacional

Nachos . . . How can one dish either take you to heaven or straight to food-hell? Where I live (El Paso–Juarez), nachos run the entire gamut of designs, from the truly authentic "botana" served with margaritas to those ballpark and movie nachos (you know, the round chips with hot "nacho cheese" pumped out of a #10 can) and everything in between.

I am a lifelong dedicated nacho eater, and to this very day there is something so deliciously wonderful about the perfecto nacho. I like to hit a 1940s place in Juarez called Martino's for dinner. There, as the deluxe appetizer before dinner, they bring you, along with your fresh Mexican key lime margarita, a botana—one plate of nachos. They fry (yes, in beef lard) homemade tortillas, top with refried beans (yes, fried in beef lard), and top with a white Chihuahua cheese. All that is crowned with a fresh jalapeño wheel and broiled; fresh guacamole is a dollar extra. The perfect bite.

Now at our house, nachos are dinner, appetizers, and soul food. I make 'em two ways. First, I grill off beef or chicken fajitas . . . chop the meat bite-size. Then I arrange two layers of whole thick chips, top with either refried beans (pinto or black) or whole beans, then the fajita meat, then not too much cheese (I like cheddar, or as my mom calls it, longhorn . . . I like that name too), sliced pickled jalapeños (especially the red ones), and put the whole thing under the broiler or on the grill to melt together. When it is hot and ready, I garnish on the side with sour cream, guacamole, and pico de gallo. . . . Dive on in, baby, the water's warm. Okay, the second kind of nacho we make (and the most popular) are chili parlor nachos. Get this: the perfect winter leftover food. Cover a platter with chips, pour homemade chile con carne on that, top with cheese, broil, finish with dollops of sour cream . . . yum!

UPTOWN

TUNA and Edam Melts

Wood-Smoked **Salmon**, Artichoke, and Charred Corn Nachos

Jamaican **Rum** Chicken Nachos with Ginger-Watermelon Salsa

Fiery **FAJITA-COTIJA** Nachos

Sloppy Jacks

Chinese **Firecracker** Nachos

Chile-Rubbed Sirloin and Green Chile Nachos

CHARRED CORN, Chicken, and **Avocado** Crema Nachos

Take your nachos uptown with a few simple recipes that come together fast and easy, usually in under twenty minutes. With just a skillet, some light chopping, or a quick measure 'n' mix, most of the special touches for these nachos can be prepared in advance, so all that's left is to heat 'n' eat.

NACHOS

Beefy Open-Faced Empanada Nachos

CAVIAR and CHIVE Nachos

Popcorn Shrimp Baja Nachos

Philadelphia Cheese Steak Nachos

BOMBAY Nachos with Curried Chickpeas and Tomato-Garlic Chutney

Crabmeat and Spinach Nachos

TUNA AND EDAM MELTS

makes one 12 × 18-inch tray or equivalent

For best results, use a rib from the heart of the celery stalk, one with tender leaves attached. If you're using salted chips, hold back on adding salt to this recipe, as the capers and Old Bay Seasoning (sold at the seafood counter or in the spice aisle) are plenty salty by themselves. You can use canned tuna, but I prefer the pouches of tuna because they don't need to be drained, which is important to prevent the chips from becoming soggy.

For the Tuna Salad

- 1 (7.06 ounce) pouch of tuna packed in water
- 3 tablespoons finely diced celery with leaves
- 2 tablespoons finely diced red or green onion
- 2 tablespoons finely diced green bell pepper
- 2 tablespoons good-quality mayonnaise
- 2 teaspoons fresh lemon juice
- 2 teaspoons capers, drained and finely chopped
- 1½ teaspoons Old Bay Seasoning
- ⅛ teaspoon granulated garlic
- Freshly ground black pepper to taste

For the Nachos

- 4 to 5 ounces corn tortilla chips
- 6 to 7 ounces shredded Edam, or cheddar, Monterey Jack, or your favorite melter (about 2 cups)
- 2 tablespoons finely minced parsley (optional)

1. Combine all ingredients for the Tuna Salad in a bowl.

2. Preheat the oven to 475°F., or preheat the broiler, with the rack positioned about 7 inches from the top of the oven or the heat source.

3. Assemble the nachos: Arrange the chips on a 12 × 18-inch baking sheet or oven-proof platter. Sprinkle on half the cheese, then top with dollops of the tuna and add the remaining cheese. Grind on plenty of black pepper.

4. Bake the nachos for 5 to 7 minutes, or broil, until the cheese is melted and bubbly.

5. Garnish with minced parsley and serve.

WOOD-SMOKED **SALMON, ARTICHOKE, AND CHARRED CORN** NACHOS

makes half of a 12×18-inch tray

Good stuff! Flake the salmon into small chunks for sprinkling on the nachos. Note that this recipe makes half of the usual 12×18-inch tray of nachos. The salmon and goat cheese are intensely flavorful and a bit rich, so these are perfect nachos for an easy appetizer or when you want just a few bites. For a full tray, just double the recipe.

2 to 3 ounces corn tortilla chips

2 ounces soft chèvre (goat cheese)

3/4 cup Charred Corn (page 74)

1/4 cup coarsely chopped marinated artichoke hearts

2 ounces alderwood-smoked salmon (or other wood-smoked variety), in bite-size pieces (about 1/2 cup)

1 to 2 tablespoons fresh dill leaves

1. Preheat the oven to 475°F., or preheat the broiler, with the rack positioned about 7 inches from the heat source.

2. Assemble the nachos: Arrange the chips on a 12×18-inch baking sheet or oven-proof platter. Top with the goat cheese, followed by the corn, artichoke hearts, and finally the salmon.

3. Bake the nachos for 5 to 7 minutes, or broil, until the cheese is soft.

4. Before serving, garnish with dill.

JAMAICAN RUM CHICKEN NACHOS WITH GINGER-WATERMELON SALSA

makes one 12 × 18-inch tray or equivalent

One Halloween, a pirate-happy buckaroo arrived at my home with a flask of Captain Morgan Spiced Rum. I'm not a big fan of rum drinks, so the undrunk bottle hung around in my liquor cabinet for a few months before I discovered its true value—as a robust seasoning ingredient. Spiced rum makes a lively marinade for kebabs, jerk pork, and chicken, while a hearty splash punches up desserts and fruity salsas.

Jamaican allspice, ground ginger, lime, coconut, and a quick hit of the Captain's rum add rhythm to these nachos. (If you don't have spiced rum, use dark rum and add a pinch more allspice and ginger to the chicken.) Serve them with a cooling Ginger-Watermelon Salsa, zipped up with chile, red onion, and more lime and ginger. (Prepare the Ginger-Watermelon Salsa, page 81, from 1 to 6 hours in advance and chill until ready to use.)

For the Marinade and Chicken

- 2 tablespoons Captain Morgan Spiced Rum (or dark rum)
- 3 tablespoons unsweetened coconut flakes
- 2 tablespoons fresh lime juice
- 1 tablespoon soy sauce
- 1 teaspoon sugar
- 1/2 teaspoon ground allspice
- 1/2 teaspoon ground ginger
- 1/2 teaspoon crushed red pepper flakes
- 1 uncooked boneless, skinless chicken breast, diced into 1/2-inch pieces

For the Nachos

- 1 tablespoon canola oil
- 4 to 5 ounces corn tortilla chips
- 6 ounces shredded 4 cheese Mexican blend (about 2 cups), or use shredded cheddar
- 1 recipe Ginger-Watermelon Salsa (page 81)

1. Combine all the marinade ingredients and toss to coat the chicken. Marinate 30 minutes, stirring after 15 minutes.

2. Warm the oil in a medium skillet on high heat. Drain the chicken of excess marinade, and fry the chicken bits in the skillet until cooked through, about

5 minutes, stirring occasionally. (The chicken may be cooked to this point and refrigerated for up to 2 days before continuing.)

3. Preheat the oven to 475°F., or preheat the broiler, with the rack 7 inches from the top of the oven or the heat source.

4. Assemble the nachos: Arrange the chips on a 12 × 18-inch baking sheet or ovenproof platter. Top the chips with the cheese. Sprinkle on the cooked chicken.

5. Bake the nachos for 4 to 6 minutes, or broil, until the cheese is melted and bubbly.

6. Serve with a bowl of Ginger-Watermelon Salsa on the side.

FIERY FAJITA-COTIJA NACHOS

makes one 12 × 18-inch tray or equivalent

One advantage that Mexican melting cheeses have over cheddar and Monterey Jack is that they resist separating when heated. That is, the oil does not release or ooze out from the solids, making for less greasy nachos, quesadillas, and baked cheese dishes. Asadero, Oaxaca, queso quesadilla, and Chihuahua cheeses are all good melters with smooth, creamy texture. Asadero's slight tanginess and mildly robust flavor go well with spicy chiles and, in this case, fajitas.

Mexicans typically garnish a dish with a crumble of Cotija, which has a dry to semidry texture and a lively taste similar to feta but with its own distinctive style. You can crumble it on raw after cooking, or cook just until the Cotija nuggets brown.

• see photo on page 54 •

4 to 5 ounces sturdy corn chips

6 ounces asadero, or other melting cheese, sliced, or about 1½ cups shredded

2 ounces crumbled Cotija (about ½ cup)

½ cup chopped pickled jalapeños, or to taste

½ recipe Grilled Fajitas (page 82), thinly sliced (about 2 cups packed, or 1 pound before cooking)

Crushed red pepper flakes to taste

1 recipe Pico de Gallo (page 77) (optional)

1. Preheat the oven to 475°F., or preheat the broiler, with the rack positioned about 7 inches from the top of the oven or the heat source.

2. Assemble the nachos: Arrange the chips on a 12 × 18-inch baking sheet or oven-proof platter. Sprinkle on the asadero, then top with the Cotija.

3. Bake or broil the nachos until the asadero just starts to melt, about 3 minutes. Remove from the oven and add the jalapeños and fajita meat. Bake or broil another 2 to 3 minutes, until the asadero is completely melted.

4. Garnish with a generous sprinkle of red pepper flakes and serve with Pico de Gallo on the side, if desired.

SLOPPY JACKS

Sloppy Joes may seem old-fashioned, but they also represent comforting home cooking. In fact, these messy meals-on-a-bun are a kitchen favorite with the chef and staff at the sophisticated New York restaurant Chanterelle (a welcome break from foie gras and caviar, no doubt). In this version, Sloppy Joes become Sloppy Jacks by covering a corn chip instead of a bun under a cozy layer of Monterey Jack cheese.

For the Sloppy Joes
2 teaspoons canola or vegetable oil
1 cup diced onion
2 cloves of garlic, minced
1 teaspoon ground red chile
1 pound lean ground beef (95% lean)
3/4 cup ketchup
1 teaspoon red wine vinegar
2 teaspoons minced parsley (optional)
Salt and freshly ground black pepper to taste

For the Nachos
4 to 5 ounces corn tortilla chips
8 ounces shredded Monterey Jack (about 3 cups)
1/2 cup finely diced green bell pepper
1/4 cup finely diced red or green onion

1. Prepare the Sloppy Joe mixture: Warm the oil in a large skillet over medium-high heat. Add the onion and cook until translucent, stirring occasionally. Stir in the garlic and ground chile and cook another minute, until the garlic softens. Dump in the ground beef and cook until crumbly and no longer pink, breaking up large chunks as it cooks. Stir in the ketchup and 1/2 cup water. Reduce the heat and simmer for about 15 minutes, stirring occasionally. The mixture should be moist and glazed, neither dry nor liquidy. Stir in the vinegar, parsley, and salt and pepper. (The mixture may be made 2 days in advance; reheat before using.)

2. Preheat the oven to 475°F., or preheat the broiler, with the rack 7 inches from the top of the oven or the heat source.

3. Assemble the nachos: Arrange the chips on a 12 × 18-inch baking sheet or oven-proof platter. Sprinkle on half the cheese, then spoon on dollops of the meat mixture. Top with the remaining cheese, bell pepper, and onion.

4. Bake the nachos for 5 to 7 minutes, or broil, until the cheese melts.

ABOVE: CHINESE FIRECRACKER NACHOS, right• below: fiery fajita-cotija nachos, page 52

CHINESE FIRECRACKER NACHOS

makes one 12 × 18-inch tray or equivalent

Popular Chino-Latino restaurants dot cities from Miami to Brooklyn, and these nachos vibrantly reflect this exotic trend. In each crispy bite, the sweet heat of Szechuan cooking dances to a Latin beat. A soft blanket of melted Muenster mellows the spiciness, and the seasoned cabbage adds a crisp, sharp note. I use Lee Kum Kee Chili Garlic Sauce, but any bottled Asian chili garlic sauce will do.

For the Pork

- 1 teaspoon toasted sesame oil
- 1 tablespoon peeled, minced ginger
- 1 pound lean ground pork (95% lean)
- 2 tablespoons Chinese chili garlic sauce
- 2 tablespoons hoisin sauce
- 1 tablespoon toasted sesame seeds

For the Nachos

- 4 to 5 ounces corn tortilla chips
- 5 ounces Muenster, sliced and torn into smaller pieces, or about 2 cups shredded
- 3 ounces napa cabbage leaves, very finely sliced
- 3 to 4 teaspoons rice vinegar
- 1 green onion, chopped (white and green parts)

1. Make the Firecracker Pork: In a large skillet, warm the sesame oil over medium heat. Stir-fry the ginger until it starts to soften, about 1 minute.

2. Raise the heat to high. Dump in the ground pork, breaking it up into crumbly bits. As the pork cooks, stir in the chili garlic sauce and the hoisin sauce. Continue to cook, stirring and breaking up the pork. Add the sesame seeds. The pork will give off juices as it cooks, then the juices will start to evaporate. Cook until the pork is fairly dry on the outer surface, so the chips don't get soggy. (The pork mixture can be fried as much as a day in advance; refrigerate if not using within an hour.)

3. Preheat the oven to 475°F., or preheat the broiler, with the rack positioned about 7 inches from the top of the oven or the heat source.

4. Assemble the nachos: Arrange the tortilla chips on a 12 × 18-inch baking sheet or ovenproof platter. Sprinkle on the cheese and then the pork mixture.

5. Bake the nachos for 4 to 6 minutes, or broil, until the cheese is bubbly. While the nachos cook, toss the cabbage with the rice vinegar.

6. Serve the nachos with green onion and the seasoned cabbage sprinkled on top.

CHILE-RUBBED SIRLOIN AND GREEN CHILE NACHOS

makes one 12 × 18-inch tray or equivalent

The inspiration for these ultra-macho nachos comes from a diner in Santa Fe, New Mexico, where I was served an enormous platter of charcoal grilled steak blanketed with fire-roasted green chiles and sharp cheese. Now I make the same dish at home, cooking up enough steak for leftovers to enjoy as nachos the next day.

4 to 5 ounces corn tortilla chips
8 ounces shredded Monterey Jack (about
   3 cups)
2 roasted and peeled green chiles (page 80), or
   ½ cup canned roasted green chiles, diced
1 recipe Chile-Rubbed Sirloin (opposite), diced

3 ounces shredded 4 or 6 cheese Italian blend
   (about 1 cup)
Avocado Crema (page 72) (optional)
Chipotle Mayonnaise (page 76) (optional)
Finely sliced lettuce and chopped onion
   (optional)

1. Preheat the oven to 475°F., or preheat the broiler, with the rack positioned about 7 inches from the top of the oven or the heat source.

2. Assemble the nachos: Arrange the chips on a 12 × 18-inch baking sheet or oven-proof platter. Top each chip with a layer of Monterey Jack, followed in order by the chiles, beef, and Italian cheese.

3. Bake the nachos for 5 to 7 minutes, or broil, until the cheese is soft and bubbly.

4. Before serving, squeeze streaks of Avocado Crema and Chipotle Mayonnaise to taste over the nachos, if using, and garnish with lettuce and onions.

CHILE-RUBBED SIRLOIN

makes one steak

A single steak, diced, is enough for one tray of nachos. But don't be shy about grilling up several of these steaks for dinner (increasing the ingredients proportionally), and saving enough meat to adorn nachos the following day.

$1/2$ teaspoon salt
$1/4$ teaspoon ground red chile
$1/4$ teaspoon ground cumin
$1/4$ teaspoon granulated garlic
$1/4$ teaspoon ground cinnamon

$1/4$ teaspoon finely ground black pepper
$3/4$ pound sirloin steak
1 teaspoon olive oil
1 teaspoon soy sauce, preferably Kikkoman

1. In a small bowl, combine the salt, chile, cumin, garlic, cinnamon, and pepper. Rub the steak all over with the mix. Set aside at room temperature for 15 minutes.

2. Heat a grill or the broiler until very hot. Rub the steak all over with the olive oil and soy sauce. Grill or broil the steak very close to the heat, about 3 minutes per side, until medium rare. Set aside for 10 minutes before slicing or dicing.

ROASTED CHILES

Besides being nacho toppers, roasted chiles and sweet peppers liven up sauces, pasta, stews, and eggs, and are delicious when simply dressed with olive oil and garlic. Long green chile peppers and sweet red and yellow bell peppers are the varieties most often roasted. Of the chiles, New Mexico chiles are about 6 inches long, slender, and vividly green; Anaheim chiles look similar but are milder and grassier in flavor; and the wide-shouldered, dark green poblano chiles are commonly served diced or stuffed as chiles rellenos.

CHARRED CORN, CHICKEN, AND
AVOCADO CREMA NACHOS

makes one 12 × 18-inch tray or equivalent

Swiss cheese, nutty and slightly sweet, combines with charred corn, chunks of chicken, and colorful streaks of Avocado Crema (page 72), plus spunky chipotle chile sauce in this Uptown Nacho. The combination of flavors is classic—almost like traditional Mexican Enchiladas Suizas (made with Swiss cheese, chicken, and sour cream), and maybe even better. This is one of my favorite dinner or full-meal nachos. Be sure to use a Swiss cheese with well-developed flavor (some brands can taste like wax).

You can prepare the corn and crema in advance, and final assembly is a breeze.

4 to 5 ounces corn tortilla chips

6 ounces good-quality Swiss cheese (about 2 cups shredded, or sliced and torn into pieces)

2 cups diced cooked chicken breast

1½ cups Charred Corn (page 74)

½ to 1 teaspoon Italian seasoning

¼ cup grated Parmesan-Romano blend, or all Parmesan or all Romano (about ½ ounce)

Avocado Crema (page 72) to taste

Chipotle Mayonnaise (page 76) to taste

1. Preheat the oven to 475°F., or preheat the broiler, with the rack positioned about 7 inches from the top of the oven or the heat source.

2. Assemble the nachos: Arrange the chips on a 12 × 18-inch baking sheet or ovenproof platter. Top each chip with a layer of Swiss cheese, followed in order by the chicken, Charred Corn, Italian seasoning, and Parmesan-Romano.

3. Bake the nachos for 5 to 7 minutes, or broil, until the Swiss cheese is soft and melted.

4. Before serving, squeeze streaks of Avocado Crema and Chipotle Mayonnaise over the nachos.

ABOVE: CHARRED CORN, CHICKEN, AND AVOCADO CREMA NACHOS, left • below: popcorn shrimp baja nachos, page 64

BEEFY OPEN-FACED EMPANADA NACHOS

makes one 12 × 18-inch tray or equivalent

When I lived in the Mexican hillside town of San Miguel de Allende, my favorite bakery snacks were savory empanadas: baked turnovers filled with everything from fruit and cheese to meat and peppers. This nacho is topped with a rustic empanada-style filling of seasoned beef, bell pepper, onion, and red potatoes—sort of like a Mexican hash. (As a shortcut, you can use prepared taco meat from the supermarket.)

Tip: Dice the vegetables fairly small, about the size of corn kernels.

1 tablespoon corn or canola oil

2 medium red potatoes, diced (about 8 ounces, or 1^2/$_3$ cups)

1 cup diced onion

1 small green bell pepper, cored and diced

^{1}/$_4$ teaspoon whole cumin seed

^{1}/$_4$ teaspoon salt

16 to 20 ounces cooked seasoned beef or taco meat

4 to 5 ounces corn tortilla chips

3^1/$_2$ ounces shredded 4 cheese Mexican blend (about 1 cup)

Dressed Greens (opposite)

1. Warm the oil in a large nonstick skillet over a medium-high heat until hot. Stir in the potatoes. Cook 30 seconds. Stir in the onion and cook another 30 seconds. Stir in the bell pepper, cumin, and salt. Continue to cook until the vegetables are browned on the edges and cooked through, stirring occasionally. Transfer from the pan to a plate.

2. In the same skillet, cook the prepared beef on medium heat until it's crumbly and most of the moisture has evaporated—it should still be moist, but not liquidy. Return the vegetables to the pan and stir into the beef. Turn off the heat.

3. Preheat the oven to 475°F., or preheat the broiler, with the rack positioned about 7 inches from the top of the oven or the heat source.

4. Assemble the nachos: Arrange the chips in a single layer on a 12 × 18-inch baking sheet or ovenproof platter. Sprinkle the cheese evenly over the chips. Spoon some of the meat-vegetable mixture onto each chip.

5. Bake the nachos for 4 to 6 minutes, or broil, until the cheese is melted and bubbly.

6. Toss on the Dressed Greens and serve.

DRESSED GREENS

2 cups loosely packed shredded lettuce	2 teaspoons olive oil
1 small fistful of cilantro, coarsely chopped ($1/2$ ounce)	$1^1/_2$ teaspoons red wine vinegar
	$1/_4$ teaspoon ground red chile

1. Toss the greens and cilantro with the olive oil, vinegar, and chile.

CAVIAR AND CHIVE NACHOS

makes 16 nachos (half of a 12 × 18-inch tray)

Add a touch of class to your next party with these elegant caviar nachos. They're upscale, but take less than 5 minutes to prepare. Pass them as a cocktail hors d'oeuvre, with martinis or champagne. Watch your cooking time: These delicate chips and toppings need only 2 or 3 minutes in a 475°F. oven. I don't recommend broiling them.

Notes: Torengos are delicate, evenly shaped, concave chips, shaped in perfect tri-angles. They come stacked in plastic canisters, sold in the supermarket snack-food aisle. I prefer them for this recipe because they hold toppings neatly. They're lighter, more refined, and less salty than regular chips—just perfect for caviar and lox and other fancy ingredients.

Eight-ounce tubs of soft, flavored cream cheese are sold next to regular cream cheese in most supermarkets. This recipe uses a naturally flavored chive-and-onion variety.

Caviar doesn't have to be beluga for this nacho, unless you prefer it. I've found that American paddlefish is a good choice, but even everyday supermarket caviar works fine. Metal gives caviar an off-taste due to a chemical reaction. For best results, mix the caviar with the lemon juice in a glass bowl with a nonmetal utensil, such as a wooden or ceramic spoon. Have all the ingredients ready and chopped before assembling the nachos, so the chips don't get soggy.

1 ounce caviar (see Notes above)
1/2 teaspoon fresh lemon juice
16 Torengos chips (about 1 1/2 ounces)
2 1/2 ounces shredded 4 or 6 cheese Italian blend
  (about 1 cup)

2 ounces soft cream cheese with natural chive and onion flavors
2 tablespoons chopped fresh chives (optional)

1. Preheat the oven to 475°F., with an oven rack in the second position, about 7 inches from the top of the oven. Set aside a baking sheet with a nonstick surface or lined with a nonstick material.

2. With a wooden or ceramic spoon (*not* metal), gently mix the caviar with the lemon juice in a small nonmetal bowl.

3. Assemble the nachos: Arrange the chips on the baking sheet. Sprinkle with the shredded Italian cheese. Using your fingers or two teaspoons, place a small knob of cream cheese on top of each chip.

4. Bake the nachos for about 3 minutes, until the Italian cheese just melts and bubbles.

5. Transfer the nachos to a serving platter. Spoon a small pile of lemony caviar on top of each chip. Garnish with fresh chives, if desired.

POPCORN SHRIMP BAJA NACHOS

makes one 12 × 18-inch tray or equivalent

The crispy, batter-fried fish taco, which originated in Baja California, has become a raging success. My nacho version uses crunchy baked popcorn shrimp, which eliminates the messy breading and frying process. A layer of garlic Jack cheese cradles the shrimp, and finely shredded cabbage with a spicy dressing completes this Baja-inspired nacho: The Baja Blanca Drizzle (page 72) is a pretty close replica of the tangy white sauce served on fish tacos. I don't recommend broiling these nachos, because it scorches the shrimp. If desired, serve with salsa and lime wedges.

Note: I use half of a 1-pound, 4-ounce container of frozen SeaPak Oven Crunchy Popcorn Shrimp (other brands may be used). Follow the manufacturer's instructions for baking the shrimp in a 450°F. oven for 10 minutes. Since you'll be baking the nachos anyway, your oven is just 25 degrees away from its final nacho cooking temperature of 475°F.

• see photo on page 59 •

10 ounces frozen popcorn shrimp (see Note above)
4 to 5 ounces corn tortilla chips
7 ounces shredded garlic Jack (about 2¹/₂ cups)

1¹/₂ cups finely shredded cabbage (3¹/₂ ounces)
1 recipe Baja Blanca Drizzle (page 72)

1. Cook the shrimp according to the package instructions, baking them until they're almost done. Keep in mind that the shrimp will bake for another 4 to 6 minutes on top of the nachos.

2. Preheat the oven to 475°F., or preheat the broiler, with the rack 7 inches from the top of the oven or the heat source.

3. Assemble the nachos: Arrange the chips on a 12 × 18-inch baking sheet or ovenproof platter. Top the chips with the cheese. Sprinkle on the shrimp.

4. Bake the nachos for 4 to 6 minutes, until the cheese is melted and bubbly.

5. Meanwhile, toss the cabbage with half of the Baja Blanca. Arrange the dressed cabbage evenly over the nachos, and drizzle the remaining dressing on top.

PHILADELPHIA
CHEESE STEAK NACHOS

makes one 12 × 18-inch tray or equivalent

A classic American sandwich meets the ultimate American snack. For best results, finely dice the onions, peppers, and beef, so they brown faster and develop those crispy, dark edges that taste *soooooo* good. If you don't have leftover grilled steak on hand, deli roast beef works well, too.

• see photo on page 67 •

1 tablespoon canola or vegetable oil
1 cup chopped onion
1 cup mixed chopped red and green bell peppers
1 cup chopped cooked steak or deli sliced roast beef (about 4 ounces)

Salt and freshly ground black pepper to taste
4 to 5 ounces corn tortilla chips
3 cups shredded cheddar or provolone (about 8 ounces)

1. Prepare the vegetables and steak: Warm the oil in a large skillet over medium-high heat. Dump in the onion and stir to coat with oil. Cook the onion without stirring until the bottom edges start to brown, about 3 minutes total. Stir in the peppers and cook, stirring only occasionally, until the whole vegetable mixture is browned but not charred, another 3 to 5 minutes.

2. Push the vegetables aside and fry the beef in the same pan until browned, about 2 minutes, sprinkling generously with salt and pepper. Stir the steak and vegetables together. (This mixture may be cooked a day in advance and refrigerated; bring to room temperature or warm slightly before using.)

3. Preheat the oven to 475°F., or preheat the broiler, with the rack 7 inches from the top of the oven or the heat source.

4. Assemble the nachos: Arrange the chips on a 12 × 18-inch baking sheet or ovenproof platter. Top the chips with the cheese. Sprinkle on the steak and vegetables.

5. Bake the nachos for 4 to 6 minutes, or broil, until the cheese is melted and bubbly.

BOMBAY NACHOS WITH CURRIED CHICKPEAS AND TOMATO-GARLIC CHUTNEY

makes one 12 × 18-inch tray or equivalent

This recipe actually combines four separate recipes into one nacho platter, but stick with me here: These are easy recipes that can all be made in advance, and each cooks up quickly. Final assembly takes just 5 minutes. In fact, the chickpeas and chutney are each good enough to stand on their own and be used in other ways, such as in part of a Bombay banquet. With the golden corn chips, yellow curried chickpeas, crimson chutney, white cheese, and pale green sauce, these nachos are as festive as an Indian feast. For even more color and flavor, sprinkle on chopped fresh cilantro just before serving.

4 to 5 ounces sturdy corn chips
1 recipe Curried Chickpeas (page 76)
1 cup (1/2 recipe) Tomato-Garlic Chutney
   (page 85)

5 ounces crumbled feta cheese (about 1 cup)
1 recipe Yogurt–Green Tabasco Streaker
   (page 81)

1. Preheat the oven to 475°F., or preheat the broiler, with the rack 7 inches from the top of the oven or the heat source.

2. Assemble the nachos: Arrange the chips on a 12 × 18-inch baking sheet or oven-proof platter. Gently mash or drop a spoonful of Curried Chickpeas onto each chip. Top with a spoonful of Tomato-Garlic Chutney, then crumble on the feta.

3. Bake the nachos for 4 to 6 minutes, or broil, until the cheese is melted and bubbly. (If the cheese is baking but not browning, run the nachos under the broiler for a few seconds, until the cheese takes on some color.)

4. Just before serving, squirt or splash on the Yogurt–Green Tabasco Streaker to taste.

ABOVE: BOMBAY NACHOS WITH CURRIED CHICKPEAS AND TOMATO-GARLIC CHUTNEY, left • below: philadelphia cheese steak nachos, page 65

CRABMEAT AND SPINACH NACHOS

makes one 12 × 18-inch tray or equivalent

If people try to tell you that nachos are only cowpoke food, stick some of these in their mouths. Rich and creamy with crabmeat, Gruyère, spinach, and a horseradish kick, they're elegant enough to serve at a black-tie affair, but just as classy at a casual barbecue. If using thin, lightweight chips, distribute the ingredients over two trays of chips instead of just one. And both the spinach-cheese mixture and the crabmeat topping may be made in advance, which makes party prep easy.

Note: For color and tangy heat, splash drops of bottled red hot pepper sauce on top. I prefer to use Frank's RedHot Sauce, the original sauce used in buffalo chicken wings, because it gives more tart, chile flavor rather than just spicy, scorching heat. Unless you live in an urban area, fresh crabmeat can be a hard ingredient to find, so use frozen or good-quality canned crabmeat if you have to; just be sure to drain it well. Finally, a busy person's spinach (leaves only) comes prewashed in 6-ounce bags. If you buy uncleaned spinach by the bunch, wash it well and remove the stems before measuring.

6 ounces fresh, well-washed spinach leaves
3/4 cup grated Parmesan or Parmesan-Romano blend
1/4 cup good-quality mayonnaise
1 green onion, finely chopped (white and green parts)
1 tablespoon prepared horseradish
1 teaspoon fresh lemon juice

1/2 teaspoon freshly ground white or black pepper
1 cup cooked crabmeat (fresh, frozen, or good-quality crabmeat in a 6-ounce can), drained
8 ounces Gruyère cheese
1 clove of garlic, coarsely chopped
4 to 5 ounces corn tortilla chips
Frank's RedHot Sauce, or other red chile sauce

1. Prepare the spinach: Cook in a dry skillet on the stove over medium heat. Or microwave in a microwave-safe container on high for 1 minute. Stir the leaves around. Microwave on high or cook in the skillet another minute, then stir and cook 1 more minute, or until the leaves are completely cooked but not dried out. Let cool, then squeeze out the liquid. When squeezed, the spinach will reduce to a ball a bit larger than the size of a golf ball (more like a Hacky Sack ball).

2. Prepare the crab mixture: Combine ½ cup of the grated Parmesan with the mayonnaise, green onion, horseradish, lemon juice, and pepper. Gently stir in the crabmeat. (This mixture can be made ahead and refrigerated for use later in the day.)

3. Prepare the cheese topping: If using a food processor, cut the Gruyère into 1-to-2-inch chunks. Place the cheese, garlic, and squeezed-dry spinach in the work bowl. Process using the steel blade until the mixture is evenly chopped and resembles small, coarse pebbles. Without a food processor, coarsely shred the Gruyère using a hand grater, mince the garlic, and finely chop the squeezed spinach, then combine these ingredients until well mixed. (This mixture can be made ahead and refrigerated for use later in the day.)

4. Assemble the nachos: Arrange the chips in a single layer on a 12 × 18-inch baking sheet or ovenproof platter. Sprinkle the cheese-spinach mixture evenly over the chips. Scatter the crab mixture on top. Dust with the remaining ¼ cup Parmesan. Splash on the hot sauce to taste.

5. Preheat the oven to 425°F. with the oven rack in the center position. (Note that these nachos bake at a lower temperature than most recipes in this book.)

6. Bake the nachos for about 10 minutes, or until the cheese is completely melted and the topping looks a bit puffy. Let rest a minute or two to set before serving, but do serve warm.

SALSAS,
SPECIALTY

Baja **Blanca** Drizzle

Avocado **CREMA**

BARBECUED Chicken

Charred Corn

Chipotle Mayonnaise

Curried **CHICKPEAS**

PICO DE GALLO

Guacamole Fiesta

Dress up your nachos with these special salsas and snazzy "streakers"—sauces you squirt on using a diner-style squeeze bottle or drizzle on with a spoon—for vivid color contrasts and powerful flavor punches. This chapter also contains the backbone recipes for the specialty toppers used in Uptown Nachos, as well as recipes for typical nacho accompaniments, like guacamole and pico de gallo.

STREAKERS & TOPPERS

Fire-Roasted Chiles and Peppers

Ginger-Watermelon Salsa

Yogurt–Green Tabasco Streaker

Grilled **FAJITAS**

Italian-Seasoned Mayonnaise

Lemon-Pepper Cole Slaw

Tomato-Garlic Chutney

BAJA BLANCA DRIZZLE

makes about 1/3 cup

This is the sauce that makes traditional fish tacos, and the Popcorn Shrimp Baja Nachos (page 64), completely irresistible. But don't limit it to seafood. The sharp, tangy flavor zips up roast beef, pork, chicken, and vegetable nachos as well.

1/4 cup good-quality mayonnaise
1 tablespoon plain yogurt
1 tablespoon fresh lime juice

1 teaspoon Frank's RedHot Sauce, or other red chile sauce
1/8 teaspoon ground red chile, such as New Mexico or California chile

1. In a small bowl, combine all the ingredients, adding more ground chile or hot sauce as desired. The sauce will last four days covered and refrigerated.

AVOCADO CREMA

makes about 1 1/3 cup

If you don't have a squeeze bottle, just drizzle the crema on the nachos with a spoon.

1 ripe avocado, peeled and pit removed
1/2 cup buttermilk
3 tablespoons lime juice (from about 1 1/2 limes)

1/4 cup sour cream
1/2 teaspoon salt

1. Puree all the ingredients in a food processor or blender. Funnel into a squeeze bottle. The mixture should be thin enough to streak easily. If not, add a few drops more lime juice or buttermilk. Plug the top of the nozzle with a toothpick and chill until ready to use. The mixture will keep for two days refrigerated.

variations Add chile powder, garlic, chives, cilantro, or green chile. Puree completely or strain before funneling into the squeeze bottle.

BARBECUED CHICKEN

makes 4 boneless, skinless chicken breast halves

This recipe makes enough for three trays of nachos. Or you can cook and serve the chicken as an entrée for one or two persons the first night, reserving enough leftovers for nachos the next day. (You'll need a bit more than one chicken breast half per nacho tray.) Brining keeps the meat moist, plump, and immensely flavorful, but if you're in a hurry, it's not necessary. Brining instructions are included below.

4 boneless, skinless chicken breast halves (about 3¹/₂ to 4 pounds total), brined or not brined (see below)

2 tablespoons olive oil
¹/₂ cup prepared barbecue sauce

1. Coat the chicken breasts with the olive oil.

2. Rub the grilling rack of a barbecue grill with vegetable oil, to prevent the meat from sticking, and heat until hot. Or, preheat the broiler.

3. Grill or broil the chicken until almost cooked through, about 3 minutes per side. Baste the chicken with barbecue sauce and continue to grill on both sides until the chicken is cooked through (not pink inside, with juices that run clear).

BRINED CHICKEN

¹/₄ cup kosher salt
¹/₄ cup sugar

2 cups water
4 boneless, skinless chicken breast halves

1. In a large bowl, stir the salt and sugar into 2 cups of water until both are dissolved. Submerge the chicken in the brine and refrigerate for 45 to 60 minutes.

2. Drain and rinse under cool water. Pat dry with paper towels. The chicken may be brined, rinsed, and dried a day ahead, and refrigerated until ready to use.

73

CHARRED CORN

makes 1¹/₂ cups, enough for one full tray of nachos

Charred corn gives nachos a wonderfully smoky flavor and a visually rustic appeal. You can embellish the corn by adding other ingredients, such as diced bell pepper, ground cumin, ground chile, or garlic. But sometimes less is more. This is a good basic recipe and packs plenty of flavor, especially when combined with more highly seasoned nachos, such as the Wood-Smoked Salmon, Artichoke, and Charred Corn Nachos (page 49) or the Charred Corn, Chicken, and Avocado Crema Nachos (page 58).

If you're lucky enough to have fresh corn on hand, by all means scrape off the kernels and toss them directly into the pan. Since I make this dish all year long, I frequently use thawed frozen corn, or a good-quality canned corn, because it keeps well on the shelf and is always handy. Whichever you choose, be sure to rinse the kernels well and let them drain in a sieve until almost all the water has dripped off. The kernels should be as dry as possible, because you want them to char, not boil or steam (but it's not necessary to dry them in towels).

1 teaspoon corn or vegetable oil
¹/₂ cup diced onion

1 11-ounce can of corn, or 1³/₄ cups fresh or thawed frozen corn kernels, rinsed and well drained

1. Warm the oil in a large skillet (preferably nonstick) over medium-high heat. When hot, dump in the onion and corn. Stir to mix the ingredients, then cook in a single undisturbed layer for about 4 to 5 minutes, or until lightly charred on the bottom. Stir again and cook in a single layer for another 3 minutes, or until the kernels range from golden to charred.

2. Let cool slightly before using, or refrigerate up to 2 days and bring to room temperature before using.

ABOVE: CHARRED CORN, left • below: curried chickpeas, page 76

CHIPOTLE MAYONNAISE

makes a generous 1/2 cup

This sunny orange mayonnaise carries a touch of smoky fire from the chipotle chiles, but it won't singe you. Fire-breathers can add more of the potent chipotle to crank up the heat. If you don't have a squeeze bottle, just drizzle the mayonnaise on the nachos using a spoon. Cans of chipotle chiles in adobo sauce are sold in the Mexican food aisle.

1/2 cup good-quality mayonnaise
1 tablespoon canned chipotle chiles in adobo, with sauce

1 tablespoon fresh lemon juice (or lime juice)
Dash of salt

1. Puree all the ingredients in a food processor or blender.

2. Funnel into a squeeze bottle. The mixture should be thin enough to streak easily when squeezed from the bottle. If too thick, add a few drops more citrus juice or water. Plug the top of the nozzle with a toothpick, and chill until ready to use. The mixture will keep for 2 weeks refrigerated.

CURRIED CHICKPEAS

makes about 1 1/2 cups

If you're a curry fan, pump up the volume by using a more fiery curry powder.

• see photo on page 75 •

1 tablespoon salted butter
1/2 cup diced onion
2 cloves of garlic, minced
2 teaspoons mild curry powder

1 15-ounce can of chickpeas, rinsed and drained, or about 1 3/4 cups cooked chickpeas
1 tablespoon fresh lemon juice (from 1/2 lemon)

1. Melt the butter in a large nonstick skillet over medium heat. Stir in the onion and cook until soft and translucent, about 2 to 3 minutes. Add the garlic and curry powder. Cook and stir 1 minute or so, until the garlic just softens.

2. Reduce the heat to low. Dump in the chickpeas. With a heatproof spatula or wooden spoon, mash the chickpeas into the onion mixture. Keep cooking and mashing for about 3 minutes. You want the chickpeas to be coarsely mashed, with both a pasty and a chunky texture. Remove from the heat. Stir in the lemon juice. Use immediately, or refrigerate for up to 2 days.

PICO DE GALLO

Pico de gallo means "rooster's beak," supposedly a reference to the tiny, coarsely chopped ingredients, as if they were snipped by a bird's beak. Pico de Gallo is the essential condiment for true Tex-Mex fajitas. It's a rustic salsa that relies on fresh ingredients, so follow your taste buds rather than adhering strictly to measurements. This recipe uses green onions, but any type will do. You may also substitute lime juice for the vinegar.

• see photo on page 78 •

1 large ripe tomato, chopped
1 to 2 green onions, chopped (white and green parts)
1/2 cup chopped fresh cilantro

1 teaspoon red wine vinegar, or to taste
1 green serrano or jalapeño chile, stemmed, seeded, and minced
Salt to taste

1. In a small bowl, combine all the ingredients.

2. Chill for about 15 minutes before serving (any longer and the flavors weaken). Stir the mixture just before serving.

ABOVE: PICO DE GALLO, page 77• below: guacamole fiesta, right

78

GUACAMOLE FIESTA

makes 2 to 3 cups

On its most basic level, guacamole is simply mashed avocados with a touch of salt and chile. This is fine; there's nothing wrong with bare-bones guac. But I like to turn my avocados into a fiesta of flavors.

Here's the deal with any recipe that uses avocados: Like snowflakes, no two avocados are alike. Even if they fall off the same tree, they may differ in size, softness, color, and flavor. And a Hass avocado tastes completely different from a bacon avocado, a Fuerte, or any of the other species. Consequently, any recipe that uses avocados can never be more than a general guide. Add seasonings. Mix. Taste. Correct the seasonings. Before serving, taste and season again. If you don't like tomatoes or cilantro, leave them out. As with all cooking, no matter what the recipe calls for, spice it the way you like it.

Flesh from 2 large ripe avocados
3 tablespoons fresh lemon or lime juice
1/2 teaspoon salt
1/2 teaspoon ground cumin
1/2 teaspoon cayenne or ground red chile

1/2 cup diced onion
2 Roma tomatoes, seeded and diced
1 tablespoon chopped cilantro
1 clove of garlic, minced

1. In a large bowl, toss the avocado with 2 tablespoons of the lemon juice. Using a potato masher or a fork, mash in the salt, cumin, and cayenne. Fold in the onion, tomatoes, cilantro, and garlic.

2. Cover the bowl with plastic wrap, pressing down so the plastic adheres to the surface of the guacamole (this prevents air from discoloring it). Let the mixture sit at room temperature for 20 minutes to 1 hour to blend the flavors.

3. Just before serving, taste and correct the seasonings, adding the remaining 1 tablespoon lemon juice if needed. Serve at room temperature.

FIRE-ROASTED CHILES AND PEPPERS

With both chiles and sweet peppers, the roasting process is the same: Char them on the outside, then let them steam covered in a bowl. After a few minutes, you simply peel off and discard the skin and use the roasted flesh, now intensely flavorful. Stir the juices from roasted peppers into salsas, salads, and cooked meat toppings.

Note: Some recipes say to remove the charred skin by running the whole pepper under running water. While this method is indeed quicker and less messy, it also washes away all the intensely flavored juices. I prefer to use the strainer method described below, running my fingers under running water as they become coated with the charred skin, rather than holding the pepper under the water. This way, the chiles are cleaned without sacrificing their juices.

Tip: After peeling, you can freeze the prepared peppers in freezer bags or containers. The taste is far superior to canned peppers, and many a winter meal in my house has come together instantly with just thawed roasted chiles, cheese, and chips or tortillas, or roasted sweet peppers and pasta.

1. Heat the grill or broiler until very hot.

2. Lightly coat the chiles or peppers with nonstick spray, or wipe them with vegetable oil. (This isn't absolutely necessary, but the oil helps transfer the heat quickly and evenly, so the skin chars and blisters faster without scorching the flesh.)

3. Place the peppers on the grill, or on a pan under the broiler. Cook on all sides until the skin blisters all over, turning after each side is done. Transfer the peppers to a bowl and cover with a damp cloth or plastic wrap. Set aside for at least 15 minutes or up to 2 hours.

4. Transfer the peppers to a sieve or colander and place it over the same bowl to catch the juices. Using your fingers, peel off the charred skin (it's okay if small bits of charred skin remain, as they add flavor and color). Discard the stem, core, and seeds. Chop or shred the peppers as called for in your recipe. Refrigerate or freeze any extra roasted peppers.

GINGER-WATERMELON SALSA

makes about 3 cups

By chopping the ingredients in the order listed, your cutting board will be less messy as you go along. If a whole watermelon seems too daunting, most produce sections sell small plastic containers of precut seedless watermelon chunks all year long.

• see photo on page 83 •

1 cup chopped red onion
1 fresh jalapeño or serrano chile, or to taste, seeded and minced
1 cup fresh cilantro, chopped
1/2 cup flat-leaf parsley, chopped
3 tablespoons fresh lime juice (from 2 limes)

1/2 teaspoon ground ginger, plus extra to taste
2 cups seedless watermelon flesh, diced small (about 2 pounds with rind, or 12 ounces of chunks without rind)
Freshly ground black pepper to taste
Salt to taste

1. In a large bowl, combine the red onion, chile, cilantro, parsley, lime juice, the 1/2 teaspoon of ground ginger, watermelon, and black pepper. Refrigerate, covered, at least 1 hour and up to 6 hours to blend flavors.

2. Stir and add salt to taste just before serving, and perk up the flavors with a dash of additional ground ginger.

YOGURT–GREEN TABASCO STREAKER

makes about 1/4 cup

1/4 cup plain yogurt

2 teaspoons Tabasco Green Pepper Sauce, or to taste

1. Mix together the yogurt and Tabasco.

2. If desired, funnel into a squeeze bottle. The recipe may be made 2 days in advance. Refrigerate until ready to use.

GRILLED FAJITAS

makes enough for two 12 × 18-inch trays of nachos or equivalent

Fajitas are a pure Tex-Mex food. They originated along the Rio Grande River on the border, where they were grilled up by cattle wranglers. The skirt steak is the traditional cut, reserved especially for the chief cowboy. Other cuts of beef can be substituted, such as flank steak or sirloin, but the skirt is by far the most flavorful. Soy sauce isn't an authentic border ingredient, but it enhances the meaty taste and helps the fajitas brown more quickly. Fajitas need to cook close to a very high heat source, to sear the outside but still leave the interior a rosy pink medium rare.

½ medium onion, thinly sliced
2 teaspoons ground cumin
3 whole pickled jalapeños, chopped
  (2 tablespoons)
½ teaspoon granulated garlic
2 pounds skirt steak

⅓ cup lime juice (from 2 limes)
2 tablespoons jalapeño pickling liquid
  (the vinegar-liquid used to pickle and flavor
  jarred and canned jalapeños)
1 tablespoon olive or vegetable oil
1 tablespoon soy sauce (optional)

1. Place half of the onions in the bottom of a nonreactive dish. In a small bowl, mix the cumin, jalapeños, and garlic together, then rub the mixture on all sides of the meat. Put the skirt steak into the dish, on top of the onions. Pour the lime juice, jalapeño pickling liquid, and oil over everything, turning the meat to coat. Sprinkle the remaining onions on top of the meat. Cover and refrigerate at least 1 hour, but preferably overnight, turning once.

2. Rub the grilling rack of an outdoor grill with vegetable oil, to prevent the meat from sticking, and heat until very hot. Or preheat the broiler.

3. Pour the soy sauce onto the meat, if desired. Grill or broil very close to the heat source, 3 to 5 minutes on each side, or just until the outside is brown and slightly charred, and the inside is still slightly pink.

4. Transfer the meat to a cutting board. Set aside for 5 minutes, then cut the meat into thin strips. Serve on nachos or in flour tortillas with Pico de Gallo (page 77).

ABOVE: GINGER-WATERMELON SALSA, page 81 • below: grilled fajitas, left

ITALIAN-SEASONED MAYONNAISE

makes about 2½ tablespoons

Italian seasoning is a blend of dried rosemary, savory, marjoram, oregano, and other herbs, sold in the spice aisle. Crumble it between your fingers to better release the flavors. If you don't have Italian seasoning, substitute your own mix of dried herbs, or simply use dried oregano.

2 tablespoons good-quality mayonnaise
1 teaspoon red wine vinegar
¼ teaspoon Italian seasoning (crushed)

⅛ teaspoon freshly ground black pepper
Pinch of granulated garlic

1. In a small bowl, combine all the ingredients.

LEMON-PEPPER COLE SLAW

makes about 1 cup

This recipe produces a light and tangy cole slaw, full of fresh, crisp flavors. Besides using it as a topper, you'll be proud to serve it as a salad on its own. And it's fast: You can whip up this slaw in less than 5 minutes—about the time it takes to cook the nachos.

2 teaspoons good-quality mayonnaise
1 tablespoon fresh lemon juice
1 green onion, finely chopped (white and green parts)

½ teaspoon coarsely ground black pepper
1 cup loosely packed, finely shredded green cabbage

1. In a small bowl, combine the mayonnaise, lemon juice, green onion, and pepper. This may be done a day in advance; refrigerate until ready to use.

2. Toss the cabbage with the dressing just before serving.

TOMATO-GARLIC CHUTNEY

Inspired by a recipe for lassan chutney by Julie Sahni, I've tamed the heat in this version and added touches of cumin, salt, and sugar for balance. It's still a tad fiery, just enough to liven up milder nacho toppings. This recipe makes enough for two trays of nachos, but you can freeze half of it for later use, either as a nacho topper or to be served as a chutney.

1/4 cup canola oil

2 dried red chiles (small hot ones, like chile de arbol or cayenne), seeds and stems removed

1 teaspoon whole fennel seed

1 teaspoon whole cumin seed

8 large cloves of garlic, thinly sliced

2 14 1/2-ounce cans diced tomatoes, with juice

2 serrano chiles, stemmed, seeded, and finely chopped

3 tablespoons minced, peeled fresh ginger

2 teaspoons Dijon mustard (preferably coarse-ground)

1 1/2 teaspoons ground cumin

1/4 teaspoon sugar

1/4 teaspoon salt, or to taste

1. Warm the oil in a large skillet over medium-high heat. Drop in the dried chiles and fry until they're almost black. Remove the chiles and discard them.

2. Reduce the heat to low and carefully add the fennel seeds, cumin seeds, and garlic. Fry the mixture in the flavored oil until the garlic starts to turn a pale golden color, 1 to 2 minutes. Add the tomatoes, serrano chiles, ginger, and mustard. Cook over medium-low heat, stirring occasionally, until thick, about 30 minutes.

3. Stir in the ground cumin, sugar, and salt, and cook another 5 minutes or so, until the mixture is as thick as ketchup, but more pulpy.

4. Spoon into a container and let cool. Serve at room temperature. The chutney may be frozen (I keep 1 cup for immediate use and freeze the remainder) or refrigerated for up to 3 days.

BREAKFAST&

LOX and Cream Cheese Nachos

Morning **Migas** Wedges

Breakfast **CHORIZO AND EGG** "Nachos Grandes"

Dulce de Leche Ice Cream Nachos with Red-Hot Honey

S'more **MACHO** Nachos

Not all nachos are spiked with chiles or cheese. The nachos here are for your morning sweetheart or your evening sweet tooth—luscious ways to start the day or end the night with a crispy bite.

DESSERT NACHOS

LOX AND CREAM CHEESE NACHOS

makes 16 nachos (half of a 12 × 18-inch tray)

These colorful, tasty morsels are just as classy as the Caviar and Chive Nachos (page 62), and the two served together make quite a splashy appetizer. Lox is brine-cured, cold-smoked salmon (as opposed to hot- or wood-smoked salmon), and is typically served on bagels with cream cheese. Any cold-smoked salmon (also called Nova Scotia salmon) works well here.

Have all the ingredients ready and chopped before assembling the nachos, so the chips don't get soggy. And watch your cooking time: These delicate chips and toppings need only 2 or 3 minutes in a 475°F. oven. I don't recommend broiling them.

1½ to 1¾ ounces lox or smoked salmon
1½ teaspoons fresh lemon juice
16 Torengos chips (about 1½ ounces) (see Note, page 62)
2½ ounces shredded 4 or 6 cheese Italian blend (about 1 cup)

2 ounces soft cream cheese with natural chive and onion flavors (see Note, page 63)
4 cherry tomatoes, quartered
2 tablespoons finely chopped red onion
2 tablespoons chopped fresh chives or dill (optional)

1. Preheat the oven to 475°F., with an oven rack in the second position, about 7 inches from the top of the oven. Set aside a baking sheet with a nonstick surface or lined with a nonstick material.

2. Chop the lox into bite-size pieces. Toss them with the lemon juice in a small bowl.

3. Assemble the nachos: Arrange the chips on the baking sheet. Sprinkle the shredded Italian cheese evenly on top of the chips. Using your fingers, two teaspoons, or a pastry bag for piping, place a small knob of cream cheese on top of each chip. On top of each knob of cream cheese, place a piece of cherry tomato, and sprinkle on some of the red onion. Finish by topping each chip with some of the lemony lox, or add the lox after baking to prevent it from cooking.

4. Bake the nachos for 2 to 3 minutes, until the Italian cheese just melts and bubbles.

5. Transfer the nachos to a serving platter. Garnish with fresh herbs, if desired.

MORNING MIGAS **WEDGES**

makes one 8-inch pie pan; serves 3 as breakfast, or 4 to 6 as a snack

Okay, so these aren't true nachos, but they do use corn tortilla chips and can be eaten by hand. They're also a tasty and practical way to use up broken bits of chips.

Traditional migas are a rustic Mexican skillet dish of scrambled eggs, sautéed corn tortilla bits, onions, bell pepper, and spices, topped with melted cheese, tomatoes, and cilantro. Think of it as a Mexican quiche. This simple recipe uses the same ingredients, substituting crumbled corn chips for the tortillas, and is baked in a pie pan. Slice into wedges and serve for breakfast, lunch, or as a snack, with salsa.

Note: For convenience, instead of freshly cooked bacon you can use precooked crumbled bacon (real bacon, not fake bacon bits), sold in supermarkets.

6 large eggs
1/4 cup cooked, crumbled bacon (optional)
3 green onions, chopped (white and green parts)
1/4 cup diced green bell pepper
1/2 teaspoon chili powder or ground red chile
1/4 teaspoon ground cumin

Nonstick spray
1 cup crumbled corn tortilla chips
3 ounces shredded cheddar (about 1 cup)
1 medium ripe tomato, chopped up with a small handful of fresh cilantro, or salsa, or both (optional)

1. Preheat the oven to 350°F. with an oven rack in the center position of the oven.

2. In a medium mixing bowl, beat the eggs until blended. Add the bacon, green onion, bell pepper, chili powder, and cumin. Stir to combine.

3. Spritz the bottom and sides of an 8-inch glass or metal pie pan with nonstick spray. Dump the crumbled chips in a single layer over the bottom of the pan. Pour the egg mixture over the chips. Sprinkle the cheese over the egg mixture.

4. Bake for 20 to 25 minutes, until the egg mixture is set and the top surface puffs up slightly.

5. Let cool for about 3 minutes, then slice into wedges and serve with chopped tomato and cilantro or salsa, if desired.

BREAKFAST CHORIZO AND EGG "NACHOS GRANDES"

makes two 8-inch nachos grandes; serves 1 to 2

I ate my way through college at Casita Jorge's in Austin, Texas. I savored their spicy chorizo and egg burritos, doused with tart Pico de Gallo, as an addictive Sunday ritual before hitting the books (or, more likely, cooling off in Barton Springs). This recipe uses the same ingredients as Jorge's burritos—fried chorizo (Mexican sausage) and egg—but they're baked on a crispy flour tortilla, instead of rolled in a soft one.

If you bake just till the egg yolks are soft and runny, serve the tortilla whole, as a single "nacho grande," and eat it with a knife and fork. If you bake until the egg yolks are set, slice the tortilla into quarters, and eat as you would other nachos—with your hands.

Nonstick cooking spray or cooking oil
2 8-inch flour tortillas
2 ounces shredded cheddar cheese (about ¾ cup)
6 ounces Mexican chorizo sausage, fried until crumbly, and drained

2 large eggs, at room temperature
1 green onion, chopped (white and green parts)
1 recipe Pico de Gallo (page 77) or salsa to taste

1. Preheat the oven to 450°F. Place an oven rack in the center position. Lightly coat a 12 × 18-inch, sided baking sheet with nonstick spray or brush lightly with cooking oil.

2. Moisten your hands with water and rub the flour tortillas on both sides with water to dampen them. Place one tortilla on each half of the baking sheet.

3. On top of each tortilla, create a ring of cheese, leaving empty a half-inch border around the edge and enough area in the center to hold an egg. Top the cheese with a ring of fried chorizo. Carefully break 1 egg into the inner area of each tortilla. Bake for 8 to 10 minutes, or until the eggs have set to your taste.

4. Using a large spatula, transfer the tortillas to plates. Serve the nachos grandes whole, or if the eggs are fully set, slice into quarters. Garnish with chopped green onion and serve with Pico de Gallo or salsa.

DULCE DE LECHE ICE CREAM NACHOS WITH RED-HOT HONEY

makes two 8-inch flour tortillas; serves 4

Think of these bite-size wedges as flat ice-cream cones. They're perfect little finger food desserts, or you can plate them up fancily with whipped cream, berries, and a dusting of cocoa powder. Southwestern cooks have long used chile powder and sweets to complement each other, and the Red-Hot Honey in this recipe not only spices up the dessert, but it also helps the ice cream balls stick to the chips without rolling off. I use Häagen-Dazs or Breyers brands of Dulce de Leche; vanilla and chocolate work well here, too.

Tips: Bake the tortillas and prepare the honey at least thirty minutes in advance to allow them to cool. For easier serving, scoop out the ice cream balls with a melon baller in advance, and freeze them until you're ready to assemble the nachos.

For the Red-Hot Honey

¹/₄ cup honey
¹/₄ teaspoon ground red chile, such as New Mexico or California chile

For the Nachos

¹/₄ teaspoon ground cinnamon
1 teaspoon sugar
2 8-inch flour tortillas
   Nonstick spray
¹/₂ pint Dulce de Leche ice cream
   Cocoa powder (optional)

1. Make the Red-Hot Honey: Measure the honey into a 1-cup heatproof measuring cup. Stir in the chile. Heat in a microwave on high about 30 seconds, until the mixture just starts to bubble up (watch closely and stop immediately if the mixture starts to boil over). Stir and set aside to cool. (Be careful! The honey will be very hot.) You may also prepare the mixture in a small saucepan over medium heat.

2. Preheat the oven to 375°F. with the oven rack in the center position.

3. Combine the cinnamon and sugar in a small bowl. Spritz two flour tortillas lightly with nonstick spray. Sprinkle with the cinnamon sugar. Slice the tortillas into 8 wedges each. Arrange the wedges on a baking sheet.

4. Bake for about 8 minutes, until the edges turn toasty. Let cool. The chips may be made 2 days in advance and stored in an airtight container.

5. To serve, dab a spoonful of Red-Hot Honey on each wedge. With a small scoop (such as a melon baller), top each wedge with one or two balls of ice cream. Dust with cocoa powder, if using, sprinkled through a sieve, and serve 2 wedges per person. Or arrange the wedges on a platter and let folks eat them as finger food desserts.

variation: Sante Fe Sprinkle Why not gild the chile-lily here? Omit the cocoa powder and drizzle more Red-Hot Honey over the ice cream, then sprinkle on toasted pine nuts for extra nuttiness and a touch of old Santa Fe.

S'MORE MACHO
NACHOS

makes one 8-inch flour tortilla; serves 3 to 6

As a Camp Fire Girl, I'm not sure which part of s'mores I enjoyed more—the process of browning (or, more often, blackening) the marshmallows on skewers over an open flame and then smooshing them between chocolate bars and graham crackers, or actually eating them.

S'mores remain a popular treat for kids and a nostalgic one for adults. Nouveau s'mores have been popping up in fine restaurants coast to coast. Some establishments actually let you toast your own marshmallows at the table over small pots of red-hot coals. Even the French Laundry (which some consider America's finest restaurant) serves s'mores, albeit with premium Valrhona chocolate, made-from-scratch marshmallows, and homemade whole-wheat honey graham crackers.

Not to be outdone by s'more mania, the *Macho Nachos* version adopts the motto "the s'more the merrier." Nutty peanut butter, thinned with a touch of maple syrup, "glues" tiny marshmallows and chocolate to a flour tortilla wedge, edged with a border of crunchy, buttery graham cracker crumbs. Just 3 minutes in a hot oven for golden, pillowy, marshmallow treats. One bite and off you go down memory lane—widened and repaved, but nonetheless, a merry pathway back to younger days.

2 tablespoons nutty peanut butter
2 teaspoons pure maple syrup
3 tablespoons graham cracker crumbs
1 teaspoon unsalted butter
1 8-inch flour tortilla

Nonstick spray
20 to 30 mini-marshmallows
2 tablespoons chocolate sprinkles or semisweet chocolate chips

1. Preheat the oven to 475°F. with an oven rack in the second position, about 7 inches from the top of the oven.

2. In a small bowl, mix together the peanut butter and maple syrup.

3. In a separate small microwave-safe bowl, toss together the graham cracker crumbs and the butter. Microwave on high for 10 to 15 seconds, or until the butter is melted enough to mash into the crumbs with a fork; the mixture should resemble coarse sand. (Or melt the butter and mix it into the crumbs.)

4. Slice the flour tortilla into 6 wedges. Arrange the wedges on a baking sheet. Lightly spritz the wedges with nonstick spray. Flip the wedges over. Lightly spritz the other side.

5. Smear a layer of the peanut butter mixture on top of the wedges. Gently press the marshmallows into the peanut butter. Sprinkle the graham cracker crumbs around the edges of the wedges, as a border. Toss the chocolate sprinkles in between and around the marshmallows.

6. Bake for about 3 minutes, until the marshmallows are toasty and golden on top. The nachos will be very hot, so cool them on the tray 1 or 2 minutes before serving. Serve warm, preferably with tall glasses of cold milk or a hot cuppa joe.

INDEX